SETH

THIS BOOK
WILL MAKE YOU
UNSTOPPABLE.

LIVING IN THE ZONE

ENGAGE THE UNSTOPPABLE POWER OF THE INTUITIVE SPIRIT...

SIDNEY C. WALKER

This publication is designed to provide authoritative information in regard to the subject matter covered. It is not meant to be a substitute for hiring the services of a competent professional when expert assistance is needed.

Published by High Plains Publications

ISBN: 0-9621177-8-1

COVER DESIGN: Neerja Kakkar—ReverInc.com
INTERIOR DESIGN: Bob Schram—BookendsDesign.com
COPYEDITING: Robin Cerwonka—RCerwonka@hotmail.com

This book is dedicated to the seekers and explorers of personal growth and evolution. To those who intuitively know somewhere in the back of their mind, this is not the world we were given long, long ago. Yes, there are good parts to this world, but we have grown tolerant of far too much negativity. Negativity is a human creation which means we can change it if we want to, and that change starts with you and me. Welcome to the new world that was always here.

TABLE OF CONTENTS

Author's Notes ix

1. What Is Possible? 1

2. VAA Formula..15

3. The Breakthrough 49

4. How to Live in the Zone 63

5. Trim Tabs...89

6. Epilogue 109

Appendices..111

• Vision–Creating Questions 112

• Favorite Resources 114

• Biography 117

• Opt In to Mailing List....................................119

• Other Books by Sidney C. Walker 120

• Hire Sid as Your Coach...................................121

This book is an endeavor to answer the following two questions . . .

1. Do you ever feel as if something is holding you back from what you are really capable of but can't figure out what it is?

2. Do you ever feel as if no matter what you accomplish, there is always something missing?

- I wrote this book for myself, my coaching clients and kindred Spirits. George Lucas had a monumentally difficult time getting *Star Wars* made. There is a movie about it. People would ask him, "Why is making this movie worth so much effort?" His answer, "Because we want to watch it!" I have a similar motivation: I want to be able to read this book.

- Learning how the ego works is a challenging topic. It is complex with lots of moving parts. Yet at the same time, it is amazingly simple to learn to get in the Zone, once you see the steps. But it does take guts.

- The information in this book is not scientifically proven. Everything presented comes from my own experience of more than three decades of coaching and personal research. Science is of indisputable value. But when it comes to philosophy, psychology, and transformation, our intuitive knowing is way beyond what we can prove scientifically, and I suspect that may always be the case.

• I'm not trying to win you over to my point of view or convince anyone of anything. I am a big advocate of free will and doing what feels intuitively right. Of course, I am excited to share what I have seen work in my own life and for hundreds of my coaching clients. However, if what I'm presenting does not feel right to you for some reason, this may not be your path.

• There is a logical flow to this book, but it is more "organized stream of consciousness" than highly packaged. I have not tried to organize each topic into neat sections with lots of white space and clever graphics. I assume anyone attracted to this book is going to be of above-average intelligence and in search of useful information. Other than some limited bold and italic type, you get to decide for yourself what is important.

• Get out your Highlighter, make notes in the margins and find your favorite parts. Imagine this to be your personal workbook for a more magical life. And, I predict that what is presented in this book is simpler than whatever you're doing.

• If you read something that is not clear, skip that part and come back to it later. There is a good chance I will say something that will resolve the issue later in the book. The effectiveness of communication comes from finding the right words. There are lots of conceptual repeats using different wording to facilitate just such a breakthrough.

- I have used the word "God" and a number of popular variations in the text to represent a loving higher power and creative source. I am spiritual more than religious. I believe in a Higher Power and also think there are a lot of ways to have a relationship with that entity. So, don't let any of my spiritual references get in your way. I am sure everything I have written about is in the Bible or other religious texts. This is my interpretation. You get to have yours. The most important thing is to find what feels right to you and live it.

- Also, while I'm asking for some artistic latitude, this book came into being toward the end of the football season. I'm a guy who likes sports, so there are several football references I could not resist. For those who are not football fans, I hope you will look past the sports analogy to the essence of what is being presented.

- Which reminds me, if I say something that you don't like or don't believe, get out your black marker and redact the text like they do with top secret documents when they release them to the public. I won't mind.

- Finally, welcome to what could be the greatest breakthrough of your life. That's what this information was for me. And I feel as if I've heard it all, if you know what I mean.

1

What Is Possible?

I MAGINE WHAT OUR LIVES WOULD BE LIKE *without negativity or suffering of any kind.* Our lives would be different. The world would be greatly different. If there were no negativity, there would be nothing wrong with you. You would be perfect the way you are and no one would ever think otherwise. There would be no war, disease, sickness, hunger, starvation, murder, car accidents, etc. No more fear, worry, or doubt. The list of negative things that would not be happening is endless.

Another fascinating aspect of a reality with no negativity is that you could not fail at anything you attempted to do. Of course, there would still be a learning process. Life on planet Earth is designed to be a process of experience and learning. But without negative thoughts, feelings, and events, you would have some certainty that you would ultimately succeed at any worthwhile endeavor in a reasonable amount of time. And without negativity, the process would be similar to learning to play tennis or learning how to build a house: You know that somehow things are going to work out if you keep at it. You learn from your experiences, and there will be enough challenge to keep your interest. In fact, that is the definition of happiness from the book *Flow* by Mihaly Csikszentmihalyi. They interviewed 100,000 people from around the world asking what would it take to be happy. The answer: "A challenge big enough to be interesting but not overwhelming."

Two of the most obvious examples of the power of negativity: 80% of all new businesses fail. And in financial services sales, which has been my coaching specialty for decades, the success rate is 3% (97% fail). People fail because of a variety of forms of negativity. If there were no negativity, failure is possible, but not likely.

So, if you could live in a way that eliminated negativity from your life, you would be perfect the way you are, and you could not fail at any reasonable endeavor. *Doesn't that sound like more fun than the difficult world we live in?*

You may be saying, it sounds great, but that is a total fantasy! That is not how the world works. Or some people would even say that life would not be as interesting without the dire potential for failure and suffering. We need negativity and fear to motivate us. Otherwise, we would sit around and do nothing.

All points of view have merit. In a free society, we get to choose how we live our lives. Let's say there is a world available to you in which you don't need to experience negativity, or at least you can get the negativity in your life down to a rare occurrence. Would that be of interest to you? Does that sound like something you would like to experience?

If your answer is no, or you think I've lost my mind, you don't need to read any further. However, if your answer is "Sure, I am open" or "Tell me more," you are in the right place.

How did we get here . . .

Let me tell you a story about something that happened thousands of years ago. There is no way of proving that what I am about to tell you is true. There are many different accounts of how life got started and evolved, and there are many contradictions. So from a practical standpoint, most of us are going to go with our intuitive sense about what we think probably happened. If you ever think about it all!

Eons ago, the beings in charge were sitting around saying, "It's great to be able to snap our fingers and create whatever we want. But wouldn't it be more interesting if we could create a game to play where there would be an infinite number of challenges, endless learning, and you would never know exactly how things would turn out? A place where no matter how much you learn or achieve, there would always be 'more to go'."

Earth became a game board. You needed a piece to be in the game, so you got a body and being (the human being) to move around the board to engage in endless adventures, big and small. Everything we do is a process of thoughts, feelings, and actions toward desired results, and we are always learning from our experience. Many aspects of life are somewhat predicable, but there is always an unknown element to keep things interesting.

You could say that life on planet Earth was created as a game to play to give us something endlessly fascinating to do. Then there was another aspect added to our existence, which was internal guidance. We were guided by a Higher Power through our intuitive instincts and our conscience. Yes, we had control over the choices we made, but we were making choices toward what felt intuitively right, and we had a clear awareness of what our path was.

The payoff for following God's Plan (the intuitive path) was that we were protected from negativity and suffering. We probably didn't even know what those things were in the beginning. How could we? They hadn't been invented yet, so to speak. Anyway, this wonderful way of life with no negativity and no suffering went on for thousands of years. Another way to describe what people experienced during this time was ongoing peace, love, joy, and abundance with no opposite. There were only the neutral and positive side of things; there was no negative side. (We are so accustomed to living in a world with the effects of negativity everywhere, it takes focus and creativity to imagine a world without it.)

And then one day, someone had the thought, "What would happen if I didn't follow my intuitive instincts or my conscience? What if I decided on my own what I wanted to do and did that?" In other words, instead of checking in with my intuition or my conscience before making a choice, as I always do, I would simply do whatever I wanted to do, for any reason that occurs to me! Or, what if I decided to not do what God wants me to do anymore and do whatever I want to do instead?

As you can imagine, this was pure folly to the majority of people at the time. Who would ever think of or want not to follow your intuitive instincts and continue to have the amazing life that you had been given.

Well, not only did it happen, it became popular. Doing your own thing instead of following God's Plan became the choice for most people over time. It's worth taking a moment to ponder. The thought that created the idea of "not God" changed everything and over thousands of years became the source of most of what the world is today.

At that point, where we separated from following our intuitive instincts and our conscience, a new self was formed. It was called the *ego*. *It was separated from God and Spirit because it was "not God."*

As you could imagine, along with this departure came a tremendous amount of fear and guilt (a new experience) that God would be upset and punish the people who made this choice. On top of that, separating from God meant you had to fend for yourself. No more internal guidance about what to do from the Source that would keep you out of trouble. You were on your own. This subsequently created a creature that was obsessed with trying to survive in a world full of unknowns that now included many dangerous traps and snares. So, the ego self soon became obsessed with learning everything it could about survival and then judging and evaluating good and bad approaches based on its experience. You had to do things a certain way or there would be negative consequences that did not exist before. You could fail, you could get hurt, you could starve, you could get an unknown "dis-ease." And, one more thing, now you could be killed or die at any time, which was not the case before.

In essence, people went from a life of peace, love, joy, and abundance with no negativity or suffering to a life of being obsessed with trying to survive in a world full of new, negative things that could happen without warning.

The most noteworthy event that changed everything for the worse was the creation of the separated ego (pseudo self) and its negativity. Some say that occurred at the point we separated from one entity and became many; some people panicked and became fearful and guilty for disconnecting from God. In the Adam-and-Eve version, which seems to have taken place after the ego was created, you had the choice of eating from the Tree of Life (intuitive Spirit) or the tree of Good AND Evil (the ego). Bottom line: The ego was not always there, negativity was not always there, and the world changed in a life-and-death negative way with the birth of the ego.

The ego is currently defined in the dictionary as "a person's sense of self-esteem or self-importance." This definition describes only a tiny part of what the ego really is. The definition is accurate in that the ego is focused on the individual self, the Me. The part that's missing from the dictionary definition is that the version of the self that the ego is focused on does not include the Spirit. The ego was created as a result of separating from the Spirit/God. You could say that the ego is a Godless self. I can hear some of you saying, "But don't people who are egos go to church or pray?" The answer is, of course, some do. The difference is that the ego hopes God is there because he or she wants help. But a real experience of God is not likely when you are living in the reality of the ego. By definition, the ego reality is totally separated from Spirit/God. And, many people do their best to live with one foot in each reality, which complicates things and really doesn't work very well. More on that later.

It would appear that God created negativity along with everything else. Yes, negativity is part of this reality, but it was actually humans who took what we had been given and created a negative version of it. Negativity was not part of the original reality we were given. We were protected from the dark side. Negativity and suffering did not exist before some humans said, "Let's try 'not God'," however that happened. Then the separated ego self became the reality of choice and became the way most people would live their lives. Unfortunately, most people have long forgotten there is anything but the ego reality. For most of us, we learned to accept the ego reality as the normal approach to life as young children.

The programming of the ego has been highly developed and embedded into our consciousness for thousands of years. Not to choose the limited ego reality would seem irrational or absurd. In other words, the reality we live in was created by human egos, not the Creator. Yes, God created the world, but we have so substantially altered the reality we were originally given, it would be unrecognizable to the original inhabitants. Some would say that the original reality created by God and the ego reality that we created as egos and now live in are exact opposites! That is such a big thought, it's hard to imagine. What if the majority of what we consider normal was created by fearful, controlling beings that didn't want anything to do with God?

How does the ego work . . .

The ego's main goal is to find a way to survive in a dangerous world without the help of Spirit. The classical phrase from the ego self is, "I live in the real world.

I don't believe in all that psycho-babble, mumbo jumbo."
What the ego is saying is that it has collected provable,
observable facts about how life works, and it does not
give any credence to any other source. The ego likes to
work with the analytical mind to keep things linearly
logical and predictable. The ego hates surprises and
the unknown.

Because the ego is obsessed with survival, it also likes
dominance, which greatly increases your odds of survival. If you are bigger, stronger, tougher, smarter, and
have more money, power, and influence, you are more
likely to survive. Let me add that, to the ego, being dominant is not just a good idea; it is a life-or-death matter.
You have to find a way to push your way to the top of the
food chain. It's a matter of who is going to survive, and
your ego is going to fight until its last breath to dominate
and be the survivor. Collateral damage to the well-being
of other humans and the health of our planet is totally
acceptable. The only thing that counts is your survival.
That is the logic of separated ego. If you don't survive,
why would you care about anything else?

Most of us are listening to a voice that is constantly
judging and evaluating what is going on around us and
telling us what is good and bad. Some call it the internal
critic. It's the voice that just innocently said, "What voice
is he talking about?" That is the voice of the ego that
does not want you to know it is the voice of the ego. The
ego wants you to think that its voice is just who you are,
and it's brilliant at disguising itself as your protector,
dedicated to keeping you safe in a dangerous world.

The ego wants to be the source of all the answers
to all our questions about how to make it in this world.

It has painstakingly collected lots of information about how life works. It has even inherited lots of information on how to be an ego from our parents and society. "Normal" (conventional wisdom) is a concept used by the ego to describe how things are supposed to be done. The ego likes things to be predictable and generally the same. It doesn't like things to get out of control or into areas where there could be uncertainty. The ego is obsessed with survival and keeping things the way they are. This is logical to the ego since if you have survived things the way they are for another day, then whatever happened is okay, and we should keep doing that. Whether something actually helps us or hurts us is not of great concern to the ego as long as we survive another day. Remember: survival and dominance are the goal of the ego, not personal growth, evolution, or something as unpredictable and messy as love.

The power of the ego's desire to maintain the status quo is something we can see if we look from a bigger perspective. Our ego tells us there are things wrong with what we have. So we change jobs, change cities, change houses, and change spouses. We work hard to make the money we need to buy the things we are convinced will make our lives better. The interesting part is that most of us create the same essence of our ego's beliefs no matter what we try to change. We attempt to make changes for the better, but we usually only change the look of things, not the essence. Said another way, we move to another town to start a new life and then create a new version of the same old life with new people and new things. (I am not advocating that it's pointless to try to improve your situation, just pointing out how much the ego gets in the way of any real improvement or change.)

Maintaining things the way they are becomes part of the awesome power of the ego. The ego is not only obsessed with our individual survival, it is also obsessed with its own survival, the existence of the ego. The ego has been around for tens of thousands of years. It has learned every angle and every trick about how to survive and maintain its control over us. It knows exactly what to do to keep us in check so we are not risking too much change, and more importantly, to keep us from asking too many questions about the source of the ego self and its true level of intelligence.

Your ego also does not want you to find out that it separated from Spirit eons ago. The ego does not trust anything unknown or unseen. If it isn't provable and observable with the five senses, it does not exist. The ego wants you to keep using it as a resource for how to live life even though it knows that something big is missing. The ego reality is fear based. It is fearful because it knows on some level that it left behind the far-reaching intelligence of Spirit in favor of having dominance and control over life. At the same time, the ego pretends to be the all-knowing, all-seeing voice of logic and reason. The problem is that the ego's ultimate goal is never growth. One of my favorite authors, Nouk Sanchez (more on her later), says the mantra of the ego is "Seek and do not find." As long as you keep seeking and don't find what you're really looking for, little is going to change. Life goes on with the approval of the ego self because the ego remains in control of a world in which human nature doesn't actually change. Obviously, our technology has grown exponentially but not our basic nature.

The ego wants you to stay busy earning money so you can buy more stuff that won't make any real difference in your life. You, of course, usually don't discover this truth until after you have lots of stuff you realize you don't need. But then you think, "There must be something else I need because it still feels I need something." Then, after work, the ego wants you to be totally busy with a complicated, demanding life so you don't have any time to reflect. All of that monumental effort is designed to keep you from discovering one thing: the unconditional love, the unlimited power, and the genius-level intelligence of the entity the ego left behind, the Spirit of God. For most people, the Spirit is usually the missing piece because it's also usually the only piece that's missing.

Another powerful weapon that the ego has in its arsenal is *resistance*. As we have discussed, the ego doesn't like real change. The ego says change is ok as long as nothing big really changes. So let's say you decide to do any of the following: take a course to improve yourself with the goal of being more successful; do something creative such as write an article about something you feel strongly about; take a dance class, an improv class, or a cooking class. Learn a foreign language. Learn to paint. Learn to play a musical instrument. Lose a few pounds. Get in better physical shape.

Guess what happens soon after you start your new project? Resistance. As soon as you run into any kind of situation in which you need to think differently or develop a new behavior (change a habit) or risk anything with an unknown element, *you will hear from the ego*. It says things such as this in a tone of genuine concern for your well-being: "Are you sure you really want to do this? You don't look that bad. Sure, you are a little out of shape, and you have let a few pounds sneak around your waistline. But look at Joe over there. He looks terrible.

You look way better than he does. Maybe you should rethink this project. Maybe we should do some more research before we commit to anything new."

Another observable rule of the ego is that the greater the risk or the greater the element of the unknown, the stronger the resistance. If you really want to engage the ego, try something such as public speaking, in which there is lots of potential for failure and ridicule. I can remember when I first started to speak in front of groups, my legs would shake, I would sweat, my mouth would be dry, and I would be in a general state of panic. How's that for resistance. The ego maintains that you would have to be totally nuts to want to speak in front of a group or do anything with that much potential for disaster. One of my favorite Jerry Seinfeld jokes echoes the lengths that the ego will go to keep us from taking risks. It goes like this: "Did you know that the fear of public speaking is actually bigger than the fear of death. So, what that means is that you would rather be the guy in the casket, than the guy giving the eulogy!"

I have been a peak-performance coach most of my life, coaching people in many different occupations. I have specialized in working with financial advisors partly because of the common fear of rejection related to making prospecting or sales calls. I wrote a book on the subject in 2016 titled *How I Conquered Call Reluctance, Fear of Self-Promotion and Increased My Prospecting*. I waited thirty years to write the book. In the meantime, I put in my 10,000 hours to become an expert on the subject, probably more like 50,000 hours if you count dealing with my own fear of rejection. One of the things I learned early in my life, which my ego has always hated, is that you learn the most and in the shortest amount of time if you put yourself in high-risk situations.

Getting on the telephone and making sales calls to promote whatever I am doing at the time has always been a high-risk activity for me. I am considered by many to be highly skilled as a telemarketer. I still make thousands of semi-cold calls every year to keep myself sharp and to prove I can do it. I am actually not an advocate of making cold calls in the financial services business. I just think it makes me a better coach. I have proof I can walk into the fire and conquer my demons (ego resistance). I often get the people I have called cold to thank me for reaching out to them. You would think with that level of skill and experience, I would not have any resistance to making sales calls. Not so.

My ego is predictable as I prepare to make prospecting calls. The first thing that's required is to get my office totally organized. Everything has to be in its place, with no papers or piles on my desk. My friends say I am so organized it's scary. I will let you in on a secret: All you have to do to get everything in your life organized is to threaten your ego with anything risky!

Then we, my ego and I, have to make sure I am not going to be hungry in the middle of a calling session so I have to eat something. That means I have to take the time to make the food or order it and pick it up.

Eventually, we are looking at the computer, getting ready to make the first call. As I look at the person's name, my ego is quick to tell me all about this individual. Now my ego doesn't actually know anything about this person, but it likes to take all the information it has stored from past calls and then create a fantasy composite of who this person is, paying special attention to finding reasons why I should not call him or her. My ego will say things like, "He has a bunch of designations; he is obviously successful and doesn't need a coach." Or "She is with a big company, they have lots of coaches available to them through the company, and there is no point in calling her." You get the idea. I am amazed at the creative genius of my ego at finding reasons not to call people. *I have learned to just call anyway* because my ego has no clue who people are. My experience is that the guy my ego does not want me to call often turns out to be the best call of the day! Stop and think about that for a minute. The part of your awareness that you are listening to for advice on how to do your life and to keep you safe often really has no clue about what is likely to happen. It just makes you think it knows what it's doing.

The ego has endless tactics to try to talk you out of whatever you are considering doing, especially is there is any risk involved or you are attempting real change of any kind. The ego is brilliant; it has been around for tens of thousands of years. The ego is relentless; it never gets tired or hungry, and it's watching you every waking moment. A skill that is critical to peak performance and for getting what you want in life in general is to learn to see through the smoke and mirrors of the ego's limited perception of reality and take action anyway. Lots more on that ahead.

2

VAA Formula

WE WILL GET TO HOW TO SHUT DOWN the negative effects of the ego, which is also how you start to eliminate negativity and suffering in your life. But first, let's look at a model for how to create whatever you want to create.

In the mid-Eighties, I met an important mentor by the name of Kurt Wright, who was a leading management consultant to Fortune 100 executives. We became friends and I ended up traveling with him to do his *Clear Purpose Management* retreat for the top 10 percent of the executives of Fortune 100 companies.

I learned many useful things from Kurt, plus we had a lot of fun together coaching top executives. The most important thing I learned from Kurt is what I now call the VAA Formula. This is my own version of what Kurt taught me, as I have expanded on the formula over the years.

There is a variety of words you could use for the three headings of the formula. The words I have chosen are Vision, Action, Attitude (VAA)—hence, the VAA Formula.

This is a formula for creating anything you want to create in this reality. It is profound and bulletproof. It always works, but that doesn't mean there won't be challenges along the way and lots of trial and correction.

Vision is the first part of the VAA formula

A vision can be a target, a goal, a purpose, a mission, a possibility, or any kind of desired outcome. A vision can be something you want to happen in the next five minutes or the next five years. It can be a canvas with a few colors and outlines on it while the rest is blank. Or it can be an architectural drawing with every aspect figured out in exact detail. A vision gives you a destination to move toward, like a North Star to follow in the sky or a point on the horizon.

A vision is typically something that you can see, but for those who are not as visual, it can be a feeling, a set of words, a sound, or any combination of the five senses. The concept of a vision is dynamic and limited only by the imagination of its creator.

One time Kurt said to me, "I have decided to become Governor of Colorado." We were both living in Denver at the time. I responded with a smile and a touch of disbelief, "Really?" He thought for a few seconds and then responded, "Well, probably not. But I like the way it makes me feel. It's a good vision for me."

Once you have a vision, hold that vision of what you want to create in your mind's eye or in your heart, or both, until it becomes a reality. We don't know how long this process will take, which is part of the challenge of holding the vision. There will be progress and breakthroughs as well as setbacks and failures. All the drama of human life gets performed in the process of bringing a vision into reality no matter its size or purpose.

Another important skill is to hold your vision in your mind's eye without allowing any of your own negative thoughts to have any effect. I like to surround my visions with a violet light of protection from all negativity.

Many books about the power of vision have been written, including one of my own titled *Trust Your Gut*, which has a section on vision. So, there is lots you can read if this topic interests you. For our purposes, I would like to mention a couple of concepts that will add major horsepower to your ability to manifest your vision.

One potent mental strategy is to *act as if your vision already exists*. It has been proven that your mind doesn't know the difference between something real and something imagined. It responds with similar intensity to both. So the more you imagine your vision to be real, the more your mind gets behind the idea and does its best to bring it into reality. This can take some focus and some practice. Your ego is likely to resist such an exercise. It loses interest outside of the provable.

It's important to make sure your vision feels intuitively right. If the part of your mind that sees the big picture has decided that your vision has merit, fits your values, and feels like something you are supposed to do on a profound level, you have a keeper. *You* have to determine what feels right to you; no one else can do that for you.

Then, taking it a step further, you can turn this vision into a mission or a purpose. In the Landmark Education vernacular, you "take a stand" for something that has meaning to you. You vow to do everything you can to bring this vision into reality regardless of the obstacles you may face.

In essence, you never give up. I like to add the qualifier that you never give up unless it feels intuitively right to do so. Sometimes there are things you need to give up. Only you can choose the worth of the vision and the commitment you make to it. And, if people ever try to convince you otherwise, take a closer look at *their* agenda. Ask yourself, "Why is it so important to them that I take a particular course of action?"

A list of questions designed to help you create a vision is in the Appendix: *Vision–Creating Questions* ...

The next part of the VAA formula is *Action*

Action, or *the act of doing,* is part two of the VAA Formula. Taking action is the thing that has the biggest impact on the physical world. You get a response from the Universe when you take an action; things happen, people respond.

If you are trying to bring a vision into reality, you want to take the action that is most likely going to manifest your vision. If you don't take this action, you are severely limiting your chances of success. Of course, you can get lucky and have the stars align to create a miracle in your favor, but as you know, that is not a sustainable strategy. So, let's limit our discussion to actually doing the work.

One of the most powerful strategies I have found for taking action is to *commit to doing the required activities toward bringing your vision into reality.* This is such an obvious statement that I am embarrassed to admit that I have struggled with this issue at times.

There are things in life that seem to take more forti-
tude and commitment to do than others—things such as
dieting, exercise, anything creative, anything involving
personal growth or change, and, of course, making sales
calls. That's my list; I'm sure your list would have some
variations. These kinds of activities have the potential for
making us incredibly happy if we succeed, and they are
also susceptible to resistance, procrastination, setbacks,
and failure, which we would rather avoid.

So, the more you can commit to doing the required
activities toward your vision, the more success you are
going to have. The problem is that for many of us, doing
the required activities is *simple*, but not always *easy*. It
reminds me of a comment I got from a financial advisor
I was talking to on the phone about coaching. He said,
"I don't need a coach. I know exactly what I need to do.
I just can't do it." I smiled and patiently explained that
finding a way to do the things you need to do is what a
skilled coach can help you discover.

Another way to describe the right approach to taking
action is to do what *has* to be done, not just what you
want to do. I have spent too much time in my life thinking about doing things rather than just doing them. It felt
like a good use of my time to try to figure out how to get
rid of my resistance to doing what I needed to do. Certainly, some of the ideas I came up with were valuable,
and I'm sharing them with you in this book. But much of
the time, my risk-averse ego was finding things for me to
do that seemed more interesting or easier than prospecting for new clients or writing the next chapter in my new
book. Another observation: Avoiding doing the required
activities usually slows down the process of manifesting
your vision.

I have created an important formula as a reminder that I have to do the required activities to bring my visions into reality. The formula is RAN2. "R" stands for *Required*, "A" stands for *Activities*, and "N2" stands for *Intuitively*. We have discussed the importance of doing the required activities toward your visions; the importance of doing them intuitively is covered in the next section, "Doing what feels intuitively right."

Doing *what feels intuitively right* . . .

I'm sure you can see the logic of doing the required activities toward your vision. There is usually no way around doing the required activities if you want to bring your vision into reality.

Another key element that affects the success of the VAA Formula is the need to do the required activities *intuitively*. When we take action, we lead with our intuitive instincts and use our analytical skills as needed to support the intuitive direction (instead of doing everything based on an analytical approach, which the ego prefers).

I have alluded to the importance of using your intuition to determine if your visions feel intuitively right. My experience is that if something feels right from an intuitive perspective, there is a much greater likelihood that your will is aligned with God's Will, and you are going to get more outside help from the Universe in bringing your vision into reality. So, from that perspective, determining whether an action feels intuitively right or not can have a big impact on the quality of your results. If the Universe is behind you, whatever you are working on is likely to happen a whole lot faster and with far fewer obstacles.

So, how do you know when something feels intuitively right? This is such an important aspect of bringing
your visions into reality. I am going to make a number of
key points on this topic.

Albert Einstein, considered one of the greatest minds
of human history said, *"The only real valuable thing is
intuition."* Here is a partial list of what people experience
when they listen to their intuitive instincts more than
their controlling, analytical egos: "being on a roll," "being
in the zone," being in the right place at the right time,
saying the right thing at the right time, more love, more
peace, more abundance, more self-confidence, better
health, an increased ability to make better decisions,
and more miracles!

If intuition is something of such great value, why is
it so ignored as a way to make the best possible decisions
about practically anything? *The biggest reason we do not
honor intuition is our academic obsession with the need for
observable, provable logic.* The source of this obsession
is the ego, which considers making decisions based on
hunches from unknown sources (intuition, conscience,
Spirit) pure folly or at best totally unpredictable.

*There is a logical explanation for why intuition is such
a powerful source for making better decisions.* This means
you can create a rationale for putting more trust in your
intuitive instincts. However, you have to have an open
mind and a willingness to experiment with advanced
ways of thinking and being. Your ego is never going to
want to have any part of this process. When my potential
coaching clients are deciding if they should hire me, I
usually tell them, "Your ego is never going to want to hire
a coach. Your ego is going to come up with lots of reasons

not to take the risk." Why? Because things could change.
For the worse? No, usually for the better. The ego hates
real change because it is an unknown. OMG, what will
you do if you start to operate at a peak performance level
and make alot more money in alot less time!?

Most people are familiar with the concept of "being in
the zone" in sports or doing something complicated. There
is a human ability to transcend the steps of linear logic and
the analytical ego to become one with your higher intelligence. In this state, you are guided to do things in a way
that you would never have considered in the analytical
state. This is the state of mind that Einstein is ultimately
referring to as intuition. It's where all the big breakthroughs come from.

It is important to say that the intuitive approach to
decision making does not take away from the analytical
conventional wisdom. Using your intuitive instincts adds
a powerful tool that will increase the odds of success in
your favor. The reality is that we were all intuitive as
kids, and we've been socialized to be more analytical by
our academic training and ultimately by many aspects
of our ego-dominated society.

Of course, not all of academia ignores intuition. I have
an article from Harvard Business School that states that the
more complicated the decision, the more you should include intuition because of the propensity for the intellect
(analytical/ego) to make mistakes due to its *narrow focus*.

Let's look at some more ways to be better at determining if something feels intuitively right.

Does everyone have intuition? Yes, as I mentioned,
we were all intuitive as kids, but as we get older, the voice

(or sense) of intuition gets hard to hear over the loud and dominant voice of the ego. We inherit a lack of trust for intuition early. Many of us have been taught by our parents not to trust our feelings at an early age. The statement that children are supposed to be "seen and not heard" is an indication of parental disregard for all feelings, let alone intuitive feelings. Also, most parents—most people for that matter—don't make a distinction between emotion and intuition. All feelings, other than maybe a few of the good ones, get lumped together as unpredictable and messy and are to be avoided.

Why is intuition so powerful? I can't prove what I am about to say, but my intuitive sense is that the intuitive database is massive. The answers coming from the intuitive database are the result of tapping into unlimited sources of information that span beyond our own awareness and even beyond this lifetime. Imagine that you have the acquired intelligence of everyone in your family tree at the time of conception. We could easily have the intelligence of thousands of people who came before us in our intuitive database. (The ego does not have that access.)

One of my mentors said that *your intuition is so advanced it will fill in the blanks where there is missing information and give you the best possible course of action, all things considered.* And it can do that in a few seconds! I have heard many people say that intuition is always right or will be proven to be right over time. Again, powerful statements that you will not hear about the ego's information.

What you experience with the ego is that it always thinks it's right. It will do everything it can to convince you it's right. In reality, the ego is not as confident as it would appear and *secretly hopes* it is right. It has been wrong many times before but tries to ignore that body of information. Furthermore, the ego's answers to problems or challenges are often limited in scope (not looking at the big picture) and self-centered or selfish, meaning that the ego has no concern about collateral damage to other people or things as long as your problem appears to be solved.

Back to the database discussion... The ego's database is limited to the information it has collected during this lifetime that it can remember or has access to. This is a tiny database compared to the seemingly unlimited capacity of the intuitive database. Where do you think you are going to get better answers? One of my favorite analogies related to this topic is that of playing sports such as ice hockey, football, rugby, or competitive downhill ski racing (and any other dangerous sport or activity). If you are approaching these sports with your analytical mind (your ego's best buddy), you are going to be totally ineffective and likely get seriously injured. In fast, physically dangerous sports, the only way you can do the sport and be any good (and survive) is to use the intuitive side of your brain and its capacity to process information much faster than you can think with linear analysis. You have to focus your attention on your intuitive instincts about what to do next. You don't have time to think!

Because the intuition can process millions of pieces of information per second (unlimited capacity), *there is really no limit to what you can learn to do or how good you can get at anything you focus your attention on.* If you can see what you want to accomplish or get a feel for it, you can eventually do anything if you keep at it. Your intuitive instincts will find a way to do it, often to the amazement and disbelief of the ego.

Teamwork was the original intent of the left and right brains. The left brain is analytical (linear) and processes one piece of information at a time. It is good at labeling and organizing information, but it is a plodder by design. The right brain (intuitive) is unlimited in the amount of information it can process per second. One the main reasons for the ego's distrust of an intuitive answer is that you don't get to see how the intuition came up with its answer. Even if you *could* see how the intuition came up with its answer to a question, it could take days or weeks to wade through the millions of pieces of information it can blaze through in a second. *So, interestingly, trusting your intuitive instincts requires a leap of faith!* Your ego lives in a world of observable proof through the five senses. To the ego, faith is the equivalent of believing in Santa Claus. It's ok for children.

An analogy I like to use related to left- and right-brain discussions is that your intuition is like Google maps with it's amazing capacity to zoom out and look at the whole world or zoom in on a mailbox in front of someone's house and do that in a few clicks of a mouse. The analytical mind is a magnifying glass which is great for looking at things in a narrow, focused way like measuring the miles between two points on the map. Both approaches (tools) are required to navigate life and they work much better as a team.

I used to do alot of public speaking, and one of my *favorite things to say was, "If you are all intuitive, you will have a tremendous sense of timing and direction, but you may have trouble getting things done. If you are all analytical, you may be really good at getting things done, but you may be doing the wrong thing at the wrong time."*

The reason we live in such an analytical (left-brain) society is because of the ego and its love affair with the provable and observable (control). The ego doesn't like anything unseen or unknown. Since the ego is more dominant than the intuitive Spirit in our world, our training is way more analytical than intuitive. There are exceptions, of course.

Hopefully you are starting to see the rationale behind the idea that trusting your intuitive instincts, or your intuitive Spirit, is going to give you better answers to your questions. I also understand that most of us don't have a lot of training or experience in trusting our intuitive instincts. We all have some, but most people are not very confident with the intuitive process. We have all been programmed to trust the conventional wisdom of the ego to get through life rather than the more unfamiliar genius of our intuitive instincts.

So that brings up the question "How do you get better at accessing your intuitive instincts?"

First, let's define "intuition" a little more. I have given you the functional aspects in our discussion thus far. Let's go to the big picture, and I will give you four of my favorite big-picture definitions of intuition.

1. A quiet sense of knowing that something is right or not right…
2. The internal promptings barely caught in the web of human consciousness…
3. The still, small voice…
4. The barely audible voice of Heaven…

As you can tell by these definitions, being intuitive is not an exact science. It is multi-faceted and personal. Everyone feels it individually and differently. The more your practice at becoming aware of your intuitive instincts, the better you will get at hearing the still, small voice or the other subtle ways the intuition guides us. The more you take action on what you hear, see, feel, or however it comes to you, the more confidence you will have in trusting this genius part of yourself. *The challenge is that it takes a leap of faith to trust your intuitive answers or promptings and that can take guts!*

The ego likes proof; your intuition doesn't offer any other than what has happened when you are trusted your intuition in the past.

I usually tell people who want to do more with their intuition to start small. Don't be making what you think are intuitive choices on major issues without some practice. If there are potential losses involved, if you make a mistake, you need to be careful that you don't wipe out your resources. In other words, being more intuitive does not mean you don't need to do research and due diligence. As you get more practice with this amazing process, you will learn to use your intuition to tell you when you can take a risk with your intuitive promptings and when you need more time and/or more information. Your intuition is not anti-analytical. Your intuition will actually tell you when you need to be analytical.

The ego makes it look like its analysis (provable linear logic) is superior to intuitive instincts (dreamy conclusions, seemingly without factual basis). But if the ego were not around, your intuitive mind and your analytical mind would be natural partners. They were designed to work as a team. When the ego is backing up your analytical mind, it wants to be right about its logical conclusions in a big way. To the ego, everything is a life-or-death situation, and

it will fight to be right. Of course, your ego's information
can work, but it's coming from a tiny database compared
to that of intuition. In a visual perspective on the difference in size of the two databases, the ego would be repre-
sented by a grain of sand. The intuitive database would
be the 600 miles of beach in Florida. Interestingly, most
people choose to go with the tiny ego database. Why?
Because we *survived* the last time we used it, not because
it worked particularly well. How's that for logic?

How do you develop your intuition? The answer to
this question may be different than what you might expect.
You actually can't be taught to be more intuitive. Your intuitive instincts are already there, and you have no control
over them. Or you could say they are always there, and
you don't have any input on what they have to say. What
you can learn is how to get the noise and distractions from
the ego down to a dull roar so you can hear, see, feel,
hunch, or otherwise get your natural intuitive guidance.
Learn to disengage from the ego and its constant banter-
ing, and you will begin to access your intuition again. I
will go into more detail on how to ignore the ego in the
upcoming Attitude part of the VAA formula.

The simplest way to engage your intuition is to ask it
questions. That sounds incredibly simple, and it is that
simple. Of course, your ego is going to want to jump in
with its answers to your question if it has one, so you are
not necessarily looking for an immediate answer. I like
to describe the process as *pose a question to your intuition
(Higher Intelligence) and wait for an answer.* Don't try to
figure out or push for an answer with linear logic (what
the analytical ego wants you to do); let it come to you.
Just be aware and open and listen and feel with all your
awareness. Your intuitive promptings can be very subtle

and quiet. But you will start to get them as you focus your attention in this way. *Remember, the intuitive hunches, promptings, directions, and feelings are already there; you just need to quiet down and slow down to hear them or feel them. Patience and heightened awareness are the keys.*

Sometimes I hear people say, "Go with your first response." I think that is dangerous. When you are more adept at knowing what is intuition and what is ego, you can better determine if your first response is the one you are looking for.

Two of my favorite intuition-engaging questions are:
1. What does it feel like it's time to do now?
2. Who does it feel like it's time to call now?

The second question is for sales people or people who do a lot of telephone work. You can adapt this question to anything important you do every day. Maybe "What does it feel like it's time to read now?" Or "Who does it feel like it's time to meet with now?" Be creative. Pose questions based on important things you do every day.

Make sure you ask these questions exactly as written above. If you substitute words like "supposed to" or "should" that will tend to hook the analytical ego and all its rules about what you've been programmed to do. That won't give you an intuitive answer unrelated to your programming. It takes a little practice and focus to not say, "What *should* I do now?" Or "What am I *supposed* to do now?" Or "What does it feel like I *should* do now?" Not that those questions won't ever work. As you get more advanced, it will matter less what words you use because you will know better what an intuitive answer feels like. For now, be specific with the wording and you will get more intuitive answers.

I still make a to-do list and prioritize what there is to do. But ask yourself the above intuitive questions once an hour. If you get an answer of some kind, consider taking action on it and see what happens. If you don't get an answer to your intuitive questions right then, just go back to your linear process and keep working on whatever you were doing. And continue to be open and aware. The answer to your intuitive question can come out of nowhere, at any time, regardless of what you are doing.

This reminds me of something important I stumbled onto many years ago. I had the idea to *keep a log* of all the times I acted on my intuitive instincts and what happened as a result. The results were quite astoundingly in favor of my intuition. It was also intriguing to realize that if I had not kept a log, I would have forgotten about most of these experiences. I still review many years of intuitive choices from time to time as a reminder of the power and brilliance of this part of us. As I alluded to earlier, I have long had the suspicion that the ego is somehow hiding the memory of intuitive successes as fast as possible. Intuition is the ego's biggest competitor. The ego wants you to listen to its proven logical advice about the real world of the five senses and not what the ego would call the whimsical musings of your flighty intuition from its unknown sources.

I can't say that my intuitive instincts were right every time, but certainly my intuition was right way more than it was wrong. I'm sure sometimes what I thought was intuition was probably not. And sometimes it would take a while for my intuitive choice to show its genius.

Years ago, I heard a voice in my head say, "Write the book." I said to myself, "What book?" I had never written a book before and was not sure that I had a book in me. But the voice was insistent and would not go away. So, after some research and reading a book called *Writing the Natural Way* by Gabriele Lusser Rico, I decided to give it my best shot. Her approach was highly intuitive, which felt right to me. One of the exercises was to write the title of the book in the middle of a page and then write all the things that occurred to you related to the title anywhere on that page. I did the exercise in a couple of minutes. Interestingly, I lost that piece of paper within days and then found it months later after the book had been published. That piece of paper was an exact outline of how the book turned out. That was one of my most memorable experiences about how advanced our intuitive ability really is. I outlined a book that took me six months to complete in a few minutes as if it were child's play!

I had another important intuitive experience while I was writing my first book. I would write for 4 to 5 hours a day and then find other things to do until I was ready to write again the next day. To my surprise, the first draft of my first book, *Trust Your Gut*, was written in less than two months. It was a totally intuitive creation. I just wrote whatever came to me every day. Sometimes I would write for an hour and then throw it all away. But in the next hour after that frustration, I would strike gold and would be amazed at what I was able to write. At one point, I was discouraged because I was not sure how all the different parts were going to fit together. Then I woke up with the idea to move the parts around until they felt right. And, magically, they all went together in ways I would have never thought possible. I have had that experience many times since on different projects. The lesson is to keep writing or doing what comes to you with any project.

Trust that it will all fit together at some point. And you won't be able to see how it will go together until it's time to see it!

One of my favorite concepts from the *I Ching*, a five-thousand-year-old Chinese book of philosophy that is highly aligned with the information I am presenting here, is *The Creative (God, Universe, Spirit) will often give you success in ways that the ego can not take credit for, just to keep you in touch with who is actually in charge.* In other words, success will come to you when you let go of your obsession for whatever you are seeking (definitely not the conventional wisdom of the ego reality). The thing you want so much will often appear shortly after you give up making it so important. You know there is truth to these ideas, and it also feels as if they are coming from a different reality. And I think they are.

When I ask my intuition questions, I often get in a quiet space with a yellow pad. I write a question in the center of the page, circle it, and write whatever comes to my mind all around the circle. Sometimes what comes to me are obvious answers from the ego's conventional wisdom. Then sometimes I will just start writing, and a different kind of answer will present itself, different than I expected. People ask, "How do I know if it's an intuitive answer?" Often the answer will not be related to any logical thought process. It will just appear. Other times you need to be patient because it can take time for the intuitive answer to float into your awareness. The thing to be aware of is that you will usually have some kind of feeling about the intuitive answer. There will be something about the intuitive answer that may be hard to describe, but it will feel right somehow, and not because it is logical. Logic is easy. We know when something makes sense.

Intuitive answers can be more mysterious. We may not totally understand the meaning of the answer we have been given. We may have to sleep on it or give it more time to unfold.

Often the intuitive answer to your question will appear when you are doing something totally unrelated to your question. You may be exercising or driving or cooking, and the intuitive answer to a question you asked three weeks ago will suddenly appear in your awareness. It is good to have something to write on or dictate into such as your cell phone. You never know when intuitive answers are going to show up, and you don't want to lose them. Some people have a pad and pen by their bed for this purpose. You will often get intuitive answers when you awaken after a night's sleep. It is always surprising to me how easy it is to lose track of those intuitive answers as the day progresses. I have often suspected that the ego is somehow involved in pushing away those intuitive answers as quickly as possible!

There are things you can do to increase the likelihood of access to your intuition. The left brain controls the right side of the body and vice versa. So any kind of movement syncs up the brain and balances out the functions of the two sides. Take a short walk or run an errand and park far enough away to get in a short walk. Any simple activity that keeps your conscious mind focusing on whatever you are doing can help clear a channel for intuition to come through. Writing has always been a powerful method for me. Often what happens to me in the process of writing is that I channel the intuitive version through logical parameters or guide posts. It is common for me to re-read what I have written and wonder who wrote that! I have trained myself to not write from the ego database unless that is useful or appropriate. I have practiced writing in what I call a contemplative meditative state for thousands of hours. It is great fun and highly rewarding. Sometimes it feels as if I am taking dictation from the Universe. You will find you are naturally intuitive in certain areas of our life if you start to pay attention to where you seem to have an ability to do things by feel or without thinking. This is different than a habit you may have developed that may be highly useful. There is nothing habitual about intuition. It is never the same from one moment to the next.

Meditation, prayer, any kind of play, or being creative can increase your awareness of your intuition. I have a friend who says that simply taking a shower helps. Others like being by a large body of water or on a large boat such as a ferry from which they can observe the water. Any kind of quiet, natural setting can work as well. I have done a lot of air travel. I feel I am more aware of my intuitive instincts at 30,000 feet. I think I hear my own thoughts better when I get above all the people on the ground and all the distracting thoughts of their egos!

Most important is to be open. *Open yourself up to the slightest nuance.* Intuition can be extremely quiet or subtle. Or it's there one moment and gone the next. Don't worry: If it's an important answer, it will come back. Your job is to go on with your life and continue to be patient and aware.

Pay attention to what your ego judges as random thoughts that float through your mind. We are programmed in our ego-driven society to ignore intuitive thoughts, hunches, or flashes. We have been programmed to dismiss our intuition's trying to communicate with us as errant thoughts that mean nothing, often to our detriment. *Remember, to the ego, any thought outside the world of linear logic or the perception of the five senses is from an unknown source and is considered untrustworthy.*

Marilyn Ferguson in her book *The Aquarian Conspiracy* created a brilliant example for our discussion:

> *Our plight might be compared to the long, long journey of twin sailors.*
>
> *One is a very verbal, analytical fellow; the other is intelligent but can't speak and is somewhat of a dreamer.*
>
> *The verbal analytical partner earnestly calculates with the aid of his charts and instruments. His (intuitive) brother, however, has the uncanny ability to predict storms, changing currents, and other navigational conditions which he communicates by signs, symbols and drawings.*
>
> *The analytical brother is afraid to trust his brother's advice because he can't imagine its source. Actually, the silent sailor has wireless, instantaneous access to a rich data bank that gives him a satellite perspective on the weather. But he cannot explain this complex system with his limited ability to communicate details. And his talkative, "rational" brother usually ignores him anyway.*
>
> *Frustrated, the intuitive brother often stands by helplessly while their craft sails head-on into disaster.*

Sometimes I have heard people say such things as, "I trusted my feelings and everything blew up! People hate me now and won't talk to me anymore." You have to make a distinction between emotion and intuition, which most people don't do. Telling people how you really feel about them (negative) is not intuition; it is emotion combined with an ego agenda. It is coming from the ego's trying to put people in their place. The ego wants to dominate, control, make other people wrong, and blame them for whatever happened.

To the ego, you are always innocent and everyone else is the problem. You will find that your intuitive promptings are never negative judgements. If you hear negative judgements, it's not intuition. The exception would be if something does not feel intuitively right. This is an extremely important communication from your Higher Self saying that something is not right and you should stay away. Unfortunately, you won't get any explanation from your intuition about why you should stay away. Sometimes you get a sense of what's not right, other times not. And often you will find out later why your intuition was putting up the red flag. If you are open and aware, your intuition can see and feel things your ego is never going to be aware of, and it can come to you in a second from a first impression with no other evidence. Again, the difference between the intuitive red flag that something is not right will be more vague or undefined than the negative and often petty judgement of the ego. The best approach is to become more aware and more discerning about where the information is coming from.

One other point to make about the challenge of becoming more aware of your intuition is that you will start to do things differently. This can cause problems for some of the other people in your life. As a family member, you are expected to play a certain role and be a certain way. The family is usually a collection of egos who have figured out a way to coexist. The relationships between people at the office can be similar. If all of a sudden you start doing things that feel intuitively right to you that don't fit what others expect from you, their egos are going to protest. The other egos will see this as abnormal and dangerous. There is something new happening here, and the ego does not like new behaviors; it likes the old ones. Another ego fear is that if you change and you are happier and/or more successful than before, the people in your life are going to have to adapt, and their egos don't like the sound of that.

When I am coaching a woman who works for a man and is being asked to do something she does not want to do, my advice is that she tell her boss that she cannot do this particular activity because "*it doesn't feel right.*" This is a powerful response because you are giving a good reason why you can't do something without giving any reasons to argue. Most men have difficulty with this response and will tend to back away. I now have alot of male clients who are comfortable using this same approach. For the men, this can be more of a challenge because this is not a logical response. But as my male clients have grown to trust the power and brilliance of their intuitive instincts, they find it much easier to offer this kind of response. You could also say, "I'm not sure how I feel about that. Let me get back to you..."

Attitude, the third part of the VAA formula

Attitude is a powerful part of the formula. Attitude is like an ether that surrounds all things in your life. As with reading comprehension, to fully understand what is being said in a sentence, you look at the overall context of the paragraph. To understand the paragraph, you may consider the larger context of the chapter or even the context of the book.

Your attitude is the context of your life at the moment. It is an overall feeling about yourself and what you are doing that has a profound effect on the results of your thoughts and actions. In the simplest of terms, if your attitude is positive you will tend to attract positive influences and results. If your attitude is negative, you will tend to attract negative aspects.

Your attitude is a choice moment by moment although there are times when it doesn't feel that you have a choice. We have programmed responses to certain situations such as loss or grief that make us react the same way every time. We consider the programmed reaction normal. But you can actually choose to have either a positive or negative attitude under any circumstance, acknowledging there may be some powerful programming in the way. If a positive attitude adds to your life, and a negative attitude takes away, you would think the logical approach would be to have a positive attitude as much of the time as possible. But in reality, many people choose a negative expectation about many things much of the time. It seems safer not to be too optimistic. This, of course, takes away from your ability to bring your visions into reality.

If you ask someone if he or she *is* a positive person, everyone will say positive. This is actually true, he or she is a positive person when not being negative. The problem is that most people ignore the amount of the time they are negative, which leads them to conclusion that they are generally positive. For some people, they are so accustomed to having a negative attitude, they think it's positive or normal to be negative. There are even "positive thinkers" who are adept at finding positive things to say, sometimes even coupled with an aura of bravado, while they are secretly scared to death and full of doubt and worry.

My experience is that having a positive attitude is a good thing and will make your life much more enjoyable for you and the people around you. But when it comes t o bringing your visions into reality, *the degree of your positive attitude is not as important as not allowing any kind of negative attitude.* It's similar to the idea that you don't need to believe in a Higher Power for it to work on your behalf, but you do need to suspend your doubt and disbelief. In other words, you need to be open or neutral and not negatively judging to create the possibility of getting help from the Universe. As you can imagine, this is a challenge for those addicted to negativity in any form. I know: I used to be one of those people!

In Angela Duckworth's best-selling book *GRIT,* she goes into great detail based on extensive research about what makes some people succeed in certain situations in which the majority will fail or quit. Interestingly, intelligence is generally not a determining factor for those who succeed. What is more important is what she calls "grit," a combination of passion and perseverance. I have reworded slightly Ms. Duckworth's qualities of grit, trying not to change her meaning:

- You know what you want, which gives you direction and focus.
- There is nothing more important than this focus.
- You have an enduring passion for your focus, which gives you dogged perseverance and ferocious determination.
- You are hard working and resilient. You keep going after a failure, and failure has no effect on your attitude.
- You are driven to improve no matter how many obstacles you face.

Can you guess what I would say is the most important characteristic of people with grit? They don't give themselves the luxury of negative thought!

Where do negative thoughts come from anyway? Let's go back to our story about the creation of the ego. Someone said, "Let's not follow our intuitive instincts and conscience anymore. Let's do our own thing without God (substitute your preferred idiom)." There was no negativity up until that time. It hadn't been invented yet. The separation from God created a new version of self that had also not existed before: the ego. The ego then experienced a moment of fear and guilt about God's potential response and created a negative thought/feeling for the first time in history. We have been living with the resulting fear, guilt, and expectation of being treated unfairly, which has led to monumental suffering ever since.

Let's say we have some idea of the origin of negative thoughts and feelings even though there are lots of interpretations of what actually happened and it was a long, long time ago. We may never know for sure, but fortunately we have our intuitive instincts to help us find enough truth to forge ahead with our lives. So here we are: Let's look at how the ego's negativity manifests itself in our daily lives.

Some call it the negative spiral. First, something happens that appears to be in the way or an obstacle to what you want. Let's say you are running late and in a hurry to get to work. You are driving faster than normal even though it's wet and foggy. You are distracted by a text on your phone which you glance at for a second and then remember you need to focus on your driving. As you look back at the road in front of you, you see the brake lights of a stopped car just up ahead of you. You slam on the brakes and hope for the best. Alot of screeching and swearing occurs, but you still smash into the stopped car ahead of you at about 30 miles per hour. The airbag simultaneously explodes in your face at full force. You take a moment to collect yourself. You push away the airbag so you can see what happened. You realize you don't need to call the police because you just rear-ended a city cop who seemed to appear out of nowhere.

Remember the ego's job is to help us survive in a dangerous world by keeping track of what seems to work and what doesn't work based on what has happened thus far in our life. The ego is now being reminded of past failures along with future visions of discomfort and dread. It is drawing on past experiences both real and from every cop video you have ever watched in which the perp was roughed up, unfairly treated, and unjustly thrown in the slammer without a phone call.

The ego then picks its preferred negative vision of what it has decided will most likely happen in your near future, which gets instantly projected onto the screen in your mind's eye. Your reaction, actually programmed by the ego, is fear, doubt, worry, anxiety, or any combination of a myriad of negative responses. Now you have a reason to choose a negative attitude, which you do. And all that happened in just the last few seconds.

The ego then continues to pound more nails into your coffin by looking for further validation or proof that you should maintain your negative visions. If the ego can think of any other occurrences, thoughts, visions, or signs that could be seen as negative, it uses them as further proof that negative thoughts and feelings are warranted.

Before you know it, you have a collection of major proof for why you should be intensely afraid of what might happen to you.

Of course, none of these imagined and projected negative things have actually happened yet, but you are reacting as if they will happen. Being the powerful creator that you are, you are unwittingly giving energy to the creation of the negative visions that have not happened yet. Need I remind you, these negative visions don't actually need to happen if you stop giving them your creative energy. But that doesn't occur to you because the negative evidence is so overwhelming. Your ego has created a masterpiece. In reality, the only thing that has actually happened is that you rear-ended a cop car at 30 miles per hour. The rest of it, so far, is a Walt Disney fantasy complements of your well-meaning but misguided ego and its commitment to keep you safe. Hopefully you are starting to see that the resources and the intent of the ego are highly suspect at best.

An obvious question: What is the easiest way to limit the influence of the negative ego or to change your negative attitude?

The easiest way to change your attitude is to shift your perception to a bigger perspective. If you are stuck with a negative attitude or a negative judgement of some kind, it is usually the result of the ego and the analytical mind teaming up. The ego wants to be right about the information it has collected about how to survive, and the analytical mind has a highly narrow focus and does not see the big picture. So now you are stuck with a negative point of view that you may have a hard time getting rid of, and you may even feel you want to defend it to some degree. But at the same time, a negative point of view is no fun and keeps you stuck and can cause things to get even worse.

Let's say that you are short on income this month due to some circumstances that were out of your control. Your ego is going to be in a panic looking at all the negative things that could happen. So, you have a choice of being upset that you are short of money and blame whomever or whatever you think is at fault, or even swear revenge on an enemy. Your ego is now into life-and-death-level drama. Or you can shift to a bigger perspective and choose a point of view that could sound something like:

- Being short of money this month will cause some problems, but we can make it up next month.

- We have been on schedule to meet our financial goals. We can afford to take a short-term hit. This sort of thing happens and there isn't anything you can do about it. Let's keep a positive focus and not let this minor setback affect your attitude.

- If you are having a bad month, ask a different question that reflects a bigger perspective. Instead of "What kind of month are we having?" ask, "What kind of quarter can we have?"

You get the idea. Of course, you need to deal with whatever circumstances need attention, but at the same time, you want to be as resourceful as possible. Any form of negative perspective, negative attitude, or negative judgement will limit your options and the effectiveness or power of the solutions that occur to you. When you are only looking at the negative side of things and from a narrow perspective, you will not see all the options available to you. Then if you get upset or angry, get in a fight, and say things in an emotional state, you can quickly make the situation worse than it was.

Another phenomenon I alluded to earlier that takes away from your peak performance is the propensity for your dominant attitude to cause your mind to seek out and collect corresponding evidence that proves your negative attitude is warranted. In other words, when you only focus on what's wrong with the situation, you tend to find more things that are wrong. You won't see what is right. When you are focused on what is wrong and someone makes a sincere effort to try to help you, you will quickly find something wrong with that! Bottom line: Any kind of negativity, by definition, takes away from whatever you are trying to do and should be eliminated from your thinking as quickly as possible.

Remember, you get stuck with a negative attitude or a negative point of view because you are only looking at the negative side and usually from a narrow perspective of the analytical. Whenever you are stuck with a point of view you don't like, step back and look at the pros and the cons from a global perspective. You will find your attitude shifting from negative to at least more neutral if not positive. You don't need to be positive as much as you have to stop the negative. Neutral doesn't hurt anything, and some people prefer neutral. Buddhists call it the middle way. Don't let your emotions swing too far in either direction. The logic is that too much positive creates a big contrast for when things fall apart. The contrast can be a powerful negative if you are not prepared for it. I still like to pump my fist in the air and yell mightily when something good happens. I like the emotional release of it! You have to decide what works for you.

Sometimes a shift to a bigger perspective can change your perception to the point that the negative issue ceases to be a problem. Let's say you get some negative press that is not based on the truth about what actually happened. Yes, it is irritating, but you decide that it's not worth fixing the issue because you don't want to deal with the people involved. You suspect they will just keep "making you wrong" no matter what you do. So, instead of being upset about the problem, you decide to ignore it. This can take some discipline, but it's a far better strategy to let go of your ego's desire to be right, get even, or teach them a lesson. Those negative missions usually don't turn out well. It reminds me that Confucius had something to say on this topic: "Before you embark on a journey of revenge, dig two graves."

So, let's do a quick summary of the VAA Formula based on what I have presented thus far. You create a vision of what you want to create. Ideally that vision feels intuitively right to you. You then take action toward bringing your vision into reality, letting your intuitive instincts lead the way as much as possible and using analysis as a supportive tool rather than a driving force. Then you maintain a positive (or neutral) attitude by minimizing or ignoring any negative thoughts or feelings about your results.

One of the most exciting and empowering aspects of the VAA Formula is my mentor Kurt Wright's closing statement. With a twinkle in his eye, he said, "If you follow this formula, only one of two things can happen. You are either going to get the result you are trying to create, or you will get a lesson required to get the result. *Therefore, you can't lose!*" I loved the idea that you can't lose no matter what happens, good or bad, success or failure.

Another way to describe this concept is to say that once you create a vision and take action on that vision, life (God, Spirit, Universe) is actually showing you how to succeed if you pay attention to what you are being taught. The problem is that most of us have been so programmed to listen to the critical point of view of the controlling ego that we either ignore the lessons we are being given or we mercilessly beat ourselves up for our lack of results. You have heard people say, "You are too hard on yourself." That is the ego judging and evaluating everything as quickly as possible compared to its standards of analytical perfection. What often happens is we are so distracted by the rantings of the separated ego, we miss the words of encouragement from the still, small voice, which simply says, "Learn from what happened and try again."

Simplicity is a powerful thing and I recommend you dedicate yourself to seeking out the uncomplicated. Our ego programming is that nothing is simple, and much of life is hard to understand and difficult to explain. So, in the process of wandering around in the endless details, we often miss the obvious. Or we are skeptical of solutions that are not complicated. I used to carry around a lot of negative baggage from all my past failures. I was expending great mental energy trying to remember what I did wrong so I wouldn't do it again. That sounds logical at first, but it doesn't work because you are focusing on what you don't want to create!

A related common example is saying to someone, "Don't forget your car keys." People know what that communication means, but it is complicated with negativity that doesn't need to be there. We are creators. We like to create things. It is more complicated to tell your mind to *not* create something. So, the mind doesn't pay much attention to the "don't" part of the sentence. What the mind is looking for first is what to create, which turns out to be "Forget your car keys." Telling someone not to forget their car keys is more likely to send a message to the mind to forget the car keys. We are so accustomed to speaking in this more complicated negative way, we consider it normal.

The reality is that we are unknowingly making things way more complicated than they need to be and less likely to happen. Focus on what you want to create, not what you don't want to create. This is another example of how deeply entwined the negative ego is in every part of our reality. The ego has been around for thousands of years and has us convinced it is normal to speak with negative nuances. "Remember your car keys," is much more likely to create the desired result for all concerned. Your mind hears that simple, direct command with much less effort and is much more likely to remember the keys.

Two lessons from the monastery . . .

I spent ten years as a lay monk in a monastery in Long Beach, California. I didn't live in the monastery, but I lived across the street with my wife and daughter, who were also actively involved. I kept my job but spent all my free time in classes and doing service. The monastery was run by women, so it turned out to be the most advanced course on intuition I could have ever imagined. The teachings were designed for modern people, couples, and families who wanted to learn how to live as a monk in our busy material world. Everyone asks me what denomination was it. I say all of them, California eclectic.

I mention the monastery because of two lessons r elated to negativity that were key to my evolution. One time I was having a conversation with one of the top women monks (called Gopis, the Hindu word meaning "female shepherd"). I was explaining to her that my busy and powerful intellect is always trying to figure everything out and keep me safe and out of trouble. I said I was concerned that if I gave up my obsession with my critical thinking and just relied on my intuitive instincts, I might unconsciously walk out into traffic. She broke into a familiar big smile of love and understanding. She had heard different versions of this story from me before. Then she simply stated, "Your intuition would never let that happen."

My second favorite lesson on negativity came from the head of the monastery. She was a gifted woman with a powerful presence. It felt that she was living in more than one reality at a time. When you spoke with her, she was right there with you, but you could tell there was a lot more going on in her mind, as if she could see more than what you and I see. You never knew what she was going to say. And whatever it was, you learned to pay attention. There was a time when many of us were in a class and she was leading a discussion about looking back and negatively judging or feeling bad about what we had done in the past. After she listened to many of us share our thoughts on the matter, she concluded the discussion with this: "There are only two reasons to ever look back: One is to see how far you have come, and the other is if someone owes you money!"

3

The Breakthrough

W HAT I AM ABOUT TO SHARE WITH YOU **is the most powerful breakthrough of my coaching career and my life.** I have read hundreds of books, gotten to the leadership level of many cutting-edge personal growth programs, and coached thousands of people, which is the best teacher. I have been a seeker all my life although not always exactly sure what I was looking for. It reminds me of a *Dennis the Menace* cartoon I saw years ago that sums up my lifelong search. In the cartoon, Dennis is looking under the couch in the living room when his mother walks in and says, "Dennis, what are you looking for?" Dennis replies, "I don't know. But I'll know it when I see it."

This breakthrough did not come to me in a linearly logical fashion. I have become more and more intuitive in my approach to life for many years now. I seem to get a piece of the puzzle every day. It's as if someone has been giving me bread crumbs to guide me home like Hansel and Gretel. I have learned alot in the process, but nothing has ever happened to me of the magnitude of what I am about to share with you.

My breakthrough was the culmination of the influence of many sources and has been slowly evolving for a long time. A recent turning point happened when I stumbled across the author Nouk Sanchez (an Australian woman who lives in New Mexico), who has been studying *A Course in Miracles* (ACIM) for more than twenty years. I had read parts of "The Course" years ago and found it interesting. But it was like my experience of reading the Bible in that I am sure all the truth I would ever need was in those pages, but I found it hard to read and understand in many places, which lessened my enthusiasm. I have gotten more from reading other people's interpretations of such great books. I read both of Sanchez's books, *Take Me to Truth* and *The End of Death*. I highly recommend these books but with the caution that if you are not accustomed to reading advanced spiritual authors, you may need to take it slowly. Sanchez's clarity and brilliant writing allowed me to see some things that were right in front of me all the time but I had not been seeing. There were many questions that had lingered in my mind from being at the monastery for ten years. All at once, I had answers to most of my questions. One of my favorite revelations from reading Sanchez was a profound experience that there really is nothing new, only new interpretations of what has always been.

ACIM and Sanchez make the ego the villain in this reality as well as the source of all negativity and suffering. I have presented this kind of thinking in a variety of ways throughout this book, and here is the essence of my personal breakthrough. *The reality we were given eons ago, in which there were no negativity and no suffering, still exists.* It never went away. It just so happened that most people have chosen to go with the ego reality instead of the original reality we were given by our Creator. The reality we were given according to ACIM was, is, **an existence of peace, love, joy, and abundance with no opposite.** Can you imagine? No negativity. That is such an unrealistic concept, it takes some time and some imagination to consider how that would be different from the reality most of us live in now. More on that later.

I immediately started to present the idea of the existence of an alternative reality with my coaching clients, who are predominately successful, middle-aged or older financial advisors. In other words, people who have been around and made a success of their lives. I was amazed that as I shared the possibility of an alternative reality existing right next to the one we are living in, no one questioned or even resisted the idea! Of course, my clients are open, have a spiritual orientation, and are somewhat intuitive or they would not have chosen me as their coach, but still. The more I talked about the alternative reality, the more I heard things like, "Sounds good to me." Or, my favorite, "I don't have any problem with anything you've said so far. Let's keep going."

I've been teaching people leading-edge, challenging ideas for a long time. I'm not big on conventional wisdom. It has its place, but I've often found the logic of the conventional to be suspect upon further examination. (The ego likes conventional wisdom because it doesn't cause any real change.) So something you learn as a pioneer is that you have to find analogous concepts that are familiar to people to make it safe for them to venture off into the wilderness with you. My most effective analogy for the alternative reality is "being in the zone" in sports. People know what it means to "be in the zone." And, of course, it's not limited to sports. You can be in the zone as a performer, musician, surgeon, race car driver, gambler, teacher, writer, speaker, parent, lover, you name it.

What's it like when you are in the zone? You are focused in a highly resourceful state of mind. There is no negative thought. The critical chatter of the ego has disappeared. It's just you and what you are doing and an awareness of being guided about what to do from an intelligent source that you trust. You know what to do without thinking and have total confidence that your choices are the right ones for whatever you are doing. It's a magical experience that once you've had it, you want to have it again.

I smile at the end of sporting events when they ask the stars of the game how they knew what to do in the situation that changed the course of the game. They always make something up that sounds logical. In reality, they usually have no clue. They were in the zone of the moment doing what they do best without thinking, without the ego's critical chatter. I remember some years ago, LaDainian Tomlinson, who was a formidable running back for the San Diego Chargers, did an interview on *60 Minutes*. His training regimen was as tough as it gets. I got exhausted just listening to him talk about it. But then he started to talk about what it was like when he was handed the football in a game. He said he became totally focused on the feeling or sense of where he was supposed to go. In other words, there was no thought process, there's no time for that. And, the most amazing thing he said, he could not hear a thing. There was no crowd noise, just total silence. You know how loud those stadiums can be during a game. The crowd noise can affect the outcome of the game and the JumboTron is telling the fans to "Make Noise!" How's that for being in the zone?

You have your own stories to tell of times when you were in the zone. Maybe you haven't thought about it much. The ego has a way of downplaying those experiences or even tries to make us forget them. The ego does not want you to know you have that kind of power. The ego wants to be in control and be your personal hero. It doesn't want you to give any credit to some indescribable force that allows you to focus and do things you never imagined possible. Take a few moments and reflect on the times in your life when you just knew what to do and you did it. When you were so engaged in what you were doing, you lost all sense of time. Or when your awareness was so acute, everything seemed to be moving in slow motion when things were actually moving at high speed. How would you describe your experience of those moments? What did it feel like? What were you focused on? What were you aware of? What were you thinking? I profess you weren't thinking at all, just being aware and doing.

Are you ready for my breakthrough? It floated into my awareness one day as I was staring at the mountains outside my office window: **being in the Zone is the alternate reality we were originally given.** There is no ego in the Zone. You are totally in the present moment with no thought of the past or the future, which is where the ego lives. The ego doesn't know how to do the present moment because there's no critical judgement in that state of mind. You have to step out of the present moment to hear the voice of the ego and its judgements. Yes, there is some part of your brain making judgements to determine what action to take, but that happens intuitively behind the scenes. All you are aware of in the Zone is what to do next that feels right and to take action on what you are being guided to do. That is a full-time job for your mind all by itself.

The possibilities become jaw-dropping when you combine the idea of being in the Zone and living in an alternate reality where there is only peace, love, joy, and abundance with no opposite. For one thing, in that state, there is nothing wrong with you. You are perfect the way you are and there is nothing to fix. How's that for freeing up some energy? Your ego is going to have something to say about that. And here's my favorite: You can't fail at anything you attempt to do. I am not saying there isn't a process to go through to succeed. If you are in sales, there are always going to be people who don't buy. In life, there are always going to be things that work and things that don't work. Life would be too boring without that element. But overall, without negativity, you know you will eventually succeed because you are being taught to succeed by what is happening to you. And without negativity to distract you from what you are being taught, you will succeed eventually and probably in record time. Without negativity, there are no more brutal lessons and years of suffering. Whatever you set your mind to accomplish is going to work somehow.

A life in which there is nothing wrong with you and you can't fail is so different from the world we live in that it sounds like total fantasy. If you share this idea with anyone, you need to be ready for comments like, "What planet are you living on?" or "What planet are you from?" There are people who you have heard say that they would not be who they are today without the brutal lessons they have learned from devastating failure and long suffering. I am not saying that those negative experiences are not powerful. But if you could end up evolving into the same amazing person without all the trauma and drama, doesn't that sound like a more desirable alternative? If the original reality that we were given did not have negativity, there would have to be a way for us to learn and evolve into the amazing people God intended us to be without getting beat up. Said another way, in God's Original Reality, suffering was not required. Negativity and suffering are a human aberration of what we were given and are not at all required for our self-actualization.

At this point of the conversation, I am reminded of my long speaking career. Often, I would have coaching clients in the audience when I would speak. I would send my spies into the bathroom during breaks to find out how I was doing. The feedback was varied but overall consistent. One of my long-time clients and close friends said it best, "About half the people think you're a genius, and the other half think you've lost your mind!" I have a feeling that my message today would move more audience members into the "he has lost his mind" camp. But since you have read this far, you are more likely to be an advocate than a naysayer. And, it's normal to have doubts. Doubt has been my biggest barrier in life, so I know it well. More to come on that topic.

Let me give you the formula I came up with to help people stay in the Zone. I let my clients decide what they want to call the alternate reality. Some like simply "in the Zone." Others prefer, the "right-brain zone," the "intuitive zone," the "God Zone," or the "Spirit Zone." You get to call it whatever you want. The goal of this focus is to live in the alternate reality that we were originally given. It is quietly and patiently just sitting there, waiting for us to wake up and participate in a world with no negativity
ɔ suffering. This is not something you need to study
ʳs to learn how to do. You don't have to leave
ɪnd live in a cave to see the light. It's available

to everyone, right here, right now. *It's actually a simple choice, but it does take guts because it is so different from what we are used to doing.*

I call it the **PIN** Formula. The "P" stands for staying in the *present moment*. The ego has difficulty with this. Some say the ego does not exist in the present moment. The "I" stands for maintaining *the innocence of a child*. Of course, that includes having all the faculties of an adult. I am not saying become a child. And the "N" stands for *No Negativity* in any form, no negative thoughts or feelings. I don't mean to say you won't have any negative thoughts or feelings, just that you can neutralize them, shift them to the positive, or simply ignore them as soon as you are aware of their presence.

The *"stay in the present moment"* idea you have heard before. Ram Dass made famous "Be Here Now" and "The next message you need is always right where you are." You have heard people say, "All we really have is the present moment." We know what the present moment is, but we don't spend much time there. The world would not be filled with egos if we spent more time in the present moment and stopped thinking about the past or the future.

Maintaining the innocence of a child came to me one night as I was watching reruns of the TV series *Army Wives*. It's a good show to watch with one eye and do routine computer work with the other. As you can imagine, many people get buried on that show so there are alot of funerals. I was listening to a chaplain say a few words over the fresh grave of a fallen soldier. He was saying things I was familiar with, and then he said something that struck me: *"May He forgive those for their transgressions and find once again the innocence of a child."*

Then came the home run, *"For it is only with the inno-cence of child that you can enter the Kingdom of Heaven."* When I heard that, I intuitively knew that was another big piece of the puzzle. Of course, you would have to have the innocence of a child to be given the power of the Kingdom. That would be an egoless state of mind.

God doesn't want us to be egos. He, She, or They want us to be *intuitive Spirits.* The ego is trying to figure every-thing out in order to survive and work every angle in its favor to get the most for itself. If you are living in the Kingdom, there is no need for the ego, which is the ego's biggest fear. One of the teachings at the monastery was—and I am adding a little of my own vernacular—*if you are living in the Zone, you will be given what you need as you need it.* Bottom line: Maintaining the innocence of a child shuts off the ego's wily ways of working every angle to dominate and control everything in order to have more for itself. When you maintain the innocence of a child and trust what you are guided to do from a Higher Source, good things will happen beyond your ego's control and understanding. Maintaining the innocence of a child is a required focus for living in the Zone with the keys to the Kingdom while you are alive.

No Negativity is a fascinating assignment from above. This is probably the hardest of the three parts of the for-mula because negativity is so much a part of our ego reality and what we consider normal. Negativity is just a part of life, everyone knows that. That is just the way it is. Well, would you be willing to consider maybe not. My first assignment to new clients is often to have them become more aware of their negative judgements and feelings and how often they have them. For some, much of the day has some form of negativity going on. When there is no chatter in your head constantly criticizing everyone and everything, it gets quiet up there between your ears.

It reminds me of the scene in the movie *My Cousin Vinny*. Joe Pesci was the star who was accustomed to a noisy part of New York City where there was constant commotion all day and all night long. In the movie, when he found himself in a small town that was totally quiet at night, he couldn't sleep. After several days of no sleep, he could barely remain conscious when he had to represent someone as an attorney at trial the next day. Some bright soul came up with the idea to give him a cell in the local jail, where there was constant noise and interruptions all night long. He finally got a good night's sleep. The habits that we have are powerful. We have inherited some habits (ways of thinking) that have been around for hundreds, even thousands of years. It's going to take some intent and focus to stay in the alternate reality. Imagine what it was like to hear the that earth was round and not flat for the first time. How do you think you would have responded? I know my first response would have been, "No way!" That would have been my ego's response. But for everyone reading this book, you have another, quieter voice in your head that could challenge your ego with, "Not so fast. Let's hear more about this…" That would be your intuition.

I was excited to see the PIN formula and begin to put it into practice for both myself and my coaching clients. Part of me knew this was big, something I had been seeking for a long time. Part of me was incredibly excited, saying with great joy, "This is the missing piece!" Another part of me was in a state of cautious optimism, saying that it can't be that simple. How could I have missed something that obvious for so long? Actually, my biggest concern, as I let the formula waft in the room like the cedar incense I love to burn, was how could I do this if everyone else around me was being an ego? How would that work? Could it work? Could I live in the Zone and still function with everyone around me being an ego?

After a short period of panic, it occurred to me that there would have to be a transition period. The transition would not happen all at once. People who were ready would get this piece by piece. Some would get it faster than others. Some would call it all nonsense. I was familiar with all those responses. And to my amazement, as I started to talk about these ideas with people I would describe as open and somewhat intuitive, every single one said, "Tell me more." That created another surge of joy to realize that I didn't have to sell the concept of an alternative reality. There was a group of people who already knew it's there; they just needed to be reminded. They knew that what I was saying was true, or something like it was true, because they could feel it.

Here is one other piece of good news I want to share before we get into the work of how to get in the Zone and stay there as much as possible. I said earlier that God doesn't want us to be egos. There's more. There is actually an *incentive program* for those who choose to explore the alternative reality of the intuitive Spirit. The reward is miracles. Yes, the more you stay in the Zone, the more miracles you get. You can have a miracle every day. You can have more than one every day! In a world of abundance with no opposite, there is no shortage or limit on how many miracles you can have. You can create as many as you want! "What is a miracle?" you ask. You know what a miracle is. It's when things fall into place or work out in ways your ego would have never imagined possible. At the monastery, one of the teachings was *Put the Spirit first, and everything else will fall into place.* My biggest challenge so far has been to learn to accept the miracle when it happens. The ego will argue that the miracle is only luck or a fluke, that there is no Higher Power involved. To realize that a miracle is a gift of love from Upstairs for a job well done is a miracle by itself, given the dominance of the ego. A miracle is an acknowledgement that Someone is watching and that you must have done something right!

Remember that your ego, by definition, is separated from God, so your ego has no clue what God wants you to do. God's direction is going to come from your intuitive instincts. Your ego will be quick to give you its answers to your challenges, but you will usually be disappointed in the results because the ego is not really into fixing anything. The ego likes any solution to a problem that creates more problems. The ego wants to keep you stuck and suffering so that you need the ego to solve the problems it actually created for you by its negativity. *It's bizarre and somewhat frightening when you get what's really going on.* Some call it insane. We were given a flawless reality of peace and prosperity, and we turned it into a world of fear. I am not saying there are no good parts to the ego reality. The problem is that, with ego, we also have to cope with massive negativity or suffering along with the good parts of life.

What do you say we work on getting the negative parts to disappear? We don't need to fix the negative parts. That's what the ego wants us to try to do. Then we are spending our resources trying to fix what can't be fixed because every ego solution creates more problems.

The most effective approach is to disappear the negative effects of the ego rather than trying to fix the problems with ego solutions!

So, the main goal of the PIN Formula is to make you skilled at shutting down the influence of the ego. The PIN Formula shuts off the main hooks the ego uses to pull us into its web of complexity and faulty logic. You could say the PIN Formula is designed to get you to stop listening to your ego judge and evaluate everything under the sun based on its made-up and deluded rules about what is normal and acceptable. The ego separated itself from the Higher Intelligence that controls this reality. So, whatever logic the ego comes up with is going to have major holes in it. It's like a shiny new car sitting in your driveway with no gasoline. It looks good to the other egos who notice you have a new car, but it serves no other purpose than to look good in the driveway.

4

How to Live in the Zone

I T'S TIME TO JUMP INTO THE POOL *and see if you can swim in water over your head.* This is a book, so we can't actually jump into the pool, but we can imagine what it would be like. We have lots of experience of what it's like to live in the reality of the ego and to listen to our ego and all its judgements, fears, doubts, and worries. *Let's see if we can start to imagine what it would be like to live in a different reality without the ego.*

There is a scene in the Tom Cruise movie *Days of Thunder* that is a perfect reflection of where we are at this point. Characters in the movie are attempting to enter a car in the NASCAR races. They probably have enough resources to pull it off, but the key is finding a driver. The racing season has already started, and all the good drivers are taken. Enter Tom Cruise who was winning in open-wheel (Formula) races and then lost his sponsor. Cruise decides he wants to drive NASCAR and agrees to do a test run at one of the race tracks somewhere in the southeast United States.

The scene is set with the local car dealer (Randy Quaid) renting the NASCAR track and a car for $2,000

(20 minutes' worth) so Cruise can prove he can drive. The guy who can build the car is there (Robert Duvall). They have to convince Duvall that they have a driver before he will build the car. And finally, a current NASCAR driver, Rowdy Burns (Michael Rooker) with the perfectly tuned car agrees to let someone drive his car around the track as a big favor. Cruise shows up on a motorcycle as Rowdy has just taken a lap around the track and is getting out of his car.

Rowdy says, "All dialed in and ready to go." There's some argument among the other guys about whether they're going to let Cruise run the $150,000 car around the track at 200 miles per hour because he's never driven NASCAR. Duvall says, "What makes you think you can drive NASCAR?" Cruise responds, "Well I've watched it on TV, of course. You'd be surprised how much you can pick up on ESPN." Duvall responds with total cynicism, "You've watched it on TV?" Then Cruise makes a passionate plea to Duvall, "Let me run, I won't make a fool out of you." Duvall reluctantly agrees to let Cruise drive and tells him to take it easy. "It's slippery out there on turn 4."

Cruise gets in the car and is driving well at average speed. Then he tells Duvall over the radio that he's putting the hammer down. Duvall screams back, "No you're not!" Then Cruise puts it to the floor and drives the car around the 2.5 mile-track fast enough to beat the best time at the last race. As Cruise pulls the car into the pit area, one of the mechanics helps him out of the car. The mechanic says, "That was fast! You sure you've never driven NASCAR before?" Rowdy joins the conversation and says to Cruise, "You run good. Now get yourself a sponsor and let's see how you do in a crowd."

That's where we are now. You know what to do. *Now let's see how you do in a crowd.* In a NASCAR race, that means now let's see how you run with 42 other adrenaline junkies oblivious to personal peril willing to do anything to win some prize money. In our slightly less dramatic lives, it means let's see how you do with holding your vision of a new life and staying in the Zone as your ego tries to pull you back into its endless baggage.

I have had a group of coaching clients for over 20 years. They are an amazing bunch. I don't talk to them as often as I would new clients, partly because all of these people could teach the course at this point. One of these long-time clients asked me recently what I was learning from all the coaching I was doing. Great question. I should tell you this client is very analytical but has become profoundly balanced with intuition in the process of our work together over many years. My answer to him was "I have an answer for you and I want to give you fair warning; it may surprise you. (Pause, for dramatic effect.) What I have recently determined is that thinking is overrated. Do as little as possible." I thought he was going to fall out of his chair from laughing so hard.

We continued to discuss the meaning of this blinding flash of the obvious. He shared that he had noticed he had become a much better listener as he became more aware of his intuition. His work is dealing with complex financial issues and the wide variety of personalities and emotions attached to people's money. He said he used to be much more linearly logical in his explanations. He would explain things in great detail often watching people's eyes glaze over while they politely nodded as if they understood what he was saying. He still looks at all the details and thinks through to the best options, but his presentation has changed considerably. He now gives people big-picture answers with as little detail as possible. Then he sees how they do with that answer. If they need more detail, they will ask. If he senses they need more information, he tries to give them what they need. He said that he now sees that most people don't have much capacity for detail, especially related to emotional issues. They want to find a good answer to their challenge and move on to something else.

Solving a problem by looking at the details and coming up with the best options is a required part of life. But we are going to be much more effective at both finding the best options and explaining them to other people if we keep track of the big picture and not get lost in the details. This is how intuition works. *Your intuition gives you the answer you need and doesn't bother with the details.* When you get an intuitive message from within, you get the action to take, not the explanation of how the intuition came up with that particular answer. Of course, if you need more detail, we all know what to do. In some cases, you may need more time before you can make a decision. I say to my clients, "If you are not sure what feels intuitively right, you probably need more time and/or more information." Both are legitimate reasons to *stall* if you are not sure about what feels intuitively right.

As you become more focused on staying in the God Zone or the Intuitive Zone by staying in the present moment, with the innocence of a child, and basically ignoring the critical chatter of the ego, you will start to change. I find that I have become much less concerned about the future. I have lost my obsession with trying to figure everything out in an attempt to succeed or not to fail. As an ego, there is constant pressure to figure every angle, get as much information as possible, find out what other people are doing, and often put off making a decision as long as possible. There is nothing wrong with doing all that work, but why do it if you don't have to?

The more I ask my Higher Self questions and wait for the answer, the better answers I get than ever before and without all the research. I am not saying there is anything wrong with research. If it feels intuitively right to get more information, do that. But if you ask your Higher Self, your Intuitive Self, "What does it feel like it's time to do now?" and the answer is, "Take a minute and consider the options," that is what I am going to do in a peaceful, contemplative way. Sometimes, the answer that feels right is obvious, logical, and what I expected the answer would be. But other times, the intuitive answer may not be what I expected at all.

Something to consider if your goal is to grow your business (or similar): If you follow your intuitive instincts while being in the Zone, you can't fail. Somehow it is going to work. And what will work may not be what you expected. If you follow your ego and its collection of conventional wisdom, failure is statistically more likely than success. Remember, the ego does not like change.

As you learn to stay in the Zone, you naturally become more "big picture" in deciding what to do next. Most of us have had ample training on how to do the details. What we need is more practice with listening for the timing and direction of our intuitive wisdom. Sometimes you may need to find a quiet place to be and process. If you are in the middle of inescapable distractions, do your best. But if possible, take a short walk or stand up and stretch; do something to get both sides of your body moving. What I often do is put on my noise-cancelling headphones.

Sometimes the built-in white noise is enough to create some quiet. If I need a more intense buffer, I plug the headphones into my cell phone and turn on the White Noise app to *Waterfall* or *Moving Train*. There can be a party in the next room, and I won't hear any of it. I can become more aware of my internal process.

Your ego is going to let you know at some point that all this "let's find the intuitive answer" mumbo jumbo is ridiculous. You know what you need to do, and you should just do it. Of course, knowing what we need to do from a logical standpoint doesn't mean we will do it or that if we do it, it will work. Your ego will be quick to tell you what you need to do and whether you are doing it right or not. If your ego's advice doesn't work, you obviously did something wrong. It's always your fault, not the ego's.

Your ego does not have any real experience of how to do anything. What it has is movies of what has happened in the past. And it can make up movies about what it thinks will happen in the future based on movies of the past. This is the source of the ego's solutions to your problems, film. The ego quickly reviews all your relevant past experiences and then makes up what it thinks is the best approach to the current challenge. The problem with this strategy is that it usually doesn't work very well. In sports or doing anything complicated, we call this analysis paralysis. If you are thinking about how to do something correctly rather than focusing on doing what feels intuitively right in the moment, you will be distracted and your performance will suffer.

My favorite example of this is the millionaire wide receivers in a pro football game. They run down the field with blazing speed, changing direction in the blink of an

eye. The quarterback somehow throws the ball to one
perfectly, and everything looks as if it's going to be an
easy catch—until the receiver glances away for a fraction
of a second to see who is around him. He wants to pro-
tect himself, knowing he will be hit momentarily. In that
moment, the ball usually hits the receiver in the chest
and then falls to the ground for an incomplete pass, to
the dismay of the quarterback, the offense, and the fans.
The receiver was distracted for a split second by his
overly cautious ego from catching a perfect pass that
would have created a first down or changed the course of
the game. You see it every Sunday during football season!

Of course, the best receivers, who don't allow the
ego's distraction, catch the ball most of the time. I am not
saying that the desire to look to see who is going to try to
break your arm is not a logical thing to do. The defensive
backs hit as hard as they can to guarantee that your ego
is going to try to avoid being hit as you catch the ball.
So even though this is a logical thing to do, to maintain
your survival, it doesn't produce anything of value in the
game. You can't catch the ball if you are looking away to
see who is going to hit you. This is a common dilemma
presented by the ego. The ego is opting for safety first
(survival). Let's not get killed. The problem is if you don't
catch the ball, you are going to lose your job. Bottom
line, you have to risk getting hit in order to catch the ball.
The guys who risk getting hit catch the ball and become
heroes. The guys who listen to the ego and take their eye
off the ball for a split second are just a few incomplete
passes away from getting traded to another team.

Football is an extreme example of a dangerous game.
But, would you be willing to consider that the ego might
actually be an ongoing distraction for most of us, most of

the time. With the VAA Formula from Chapter 2, there are only two things that can happen if you are in the Zone. One is that you get the result you are after. Two is that you get a lesson required to get the result. *The problem is that we are usually so distracted by the critical chattering of the ego, we miss the lesson.* We don't see that life is actually teaching us how to get the thing we are after. We end up making excuses for why we didn't get what we wanted, but the reality is that we weren't paying attention to what would have created success.

We could easily double our productivity and our achievements if we listened to our intuitive instincts and focused on what we are being guided to do from our Higher Intelligence and ignore the critical chattering of the clueless ego. Some would consider that radical thinking, and it is to the ego. We have been following the advice and instruction of the ego most of our lives thinking that is just how you do it. Or, that is the way we have always done it. That describes the problem. The ego is the most brilliant player in the game at keeping us doing what we have always done even if it doesn't work. Whatever is logical and familiar is going to take priority over listening to the still, small voice of Higher Intelligence and the source of our personal genius and ultimate success.

I mentioned earlier one of my favorite questions for accessing your intuition is "What does it feel like it is time to do now?" Your analytical ego does not know how to answer this question because it doesn't do anything by feel. So, this question tends to get the attention of the right brain and intuition. You never know if you are going to get an answer from the intuitive side. Sometimes you do and sometimes you don't. If you don't get an intuitive hunch, message, prompting, feeling, there is no cause for concern. Just go back to whatever you were doing. But if you *do* get an intuitive answer like, "Call Bob," or "Go check the mail," now you have a choice to make. Are you going to trust the genius of Higher Intelligence or listen to your ego say, "That is a fleeting thought that has nothing to do with anything. Ignore it." As I said earlier, I have kept a log for many years (decades) of the times I have had an intuitive directive of some kind and took action. The results are startling. Your intuitive instincts are way ahead of your plodding analytical ego. If you follow your intuitive instincts, you are likely to find answers to problems that you would have never otherwise thought of or figured out with your intellect. When I follow my intuitive instincts, I regularly end up saying to myself, "My ego would have never seen that option!"

Of course, you can make a mistake. Mistakes are a key element of life. You can misinterpret an emotional feeling for an intuitive prompting. Maybe you get conned by your ego to go after what *feels good* rather than *what feels intuitively right*. Some call that "falling in love with the deal" as you become blinded by emotion and desire. Sometimes what feels good can also feel intuitively right, but you still need to learn the difference. My best example is that it may feel good to have another piece of that delicious pecan pie. But if you are really committed to dropping a few pounds, it won't feel intuitively right. You can see this is not an exact science. It takes practice or what I like to call "trial and correction" or "trial and adaptation." "Trial and error: has the negative ego spin.

One aspect of trusting and acting on your intuitive instincts that you can never escape is that it *takes guts*. Acting on your intuitive promptings actually requires a leap of faith because you will never have any proof that what you are being guided to do will work. Of course, the more you access your intuition and take action, you will have a growing body of evidence that shows the intuitive choice is worth trusting and usually the best possible approach, all things considered. You will start to notice that the intuitive choice will work somehow, sometimes logically but often in ways you would never imagine possible. Most important, you start to get a feel for what it's like to trust your Higher Self while your ego is screaming incredulously, "You're going to do what?" My intuition says that learning to trust our intuitive Higher Self rather than the controlling ego is one of the most important lessons we are here to learn. It's right up there with the lessons of love and forgiveness. I also suspect they are all connected somehow.

Speaking of forgiveness, this is a key element of being able to ignore the ego and live in the Zone. If there are things you have not forgiven yourself for, the ego can easily pull you back into its reality and all its negative baggage. I recommend you spend some time listing all the things you need to forgive yourself for. This takes courage. The key question is, "Can I forgive myself for that?" Your motivation is that you cannot live in the Zone if you don't find a way to forgive yourself. You will forever be the prisoner of the ego. Remember, in the original reality, there was no negative, which means there was no guilt. There is no guilt in the Zone, just space to create. So, you must find a way to forgive anything that could pull you back into the ego reality of fear and guilt. Obviously, this is a process that you do over time as you think of things to forgive. You will notice that the more you forgive yourself for, the more you will feel power coming back to you along with an increased sense of freedom to

choose whatever you are guided to do by your Higher
Self. Some say that guilt is a creation of the ego to keep
you feeling unworthy. Then you are more likely to repeat
the behaviors that created the guilt if you feel unworthy.
The ego would call that a win for its side. The ego
secretly wants to keep us right where we are. For some
people, that means being stuck on a plateau.

There are likely some people in your life (living or
past) that you need to forgive as well. There is an ancient
Hawaiian technique called *Ho'oponopono* that works well
for this purpose. Think of the people you need to forgive
and say, *"I love you, I'm sorry, please forgive me, thank
you."* Keep saying it until you can feel a shift. Look it up
on the Internet.

In the monastery, one of the head monks liked to say,
"You can't serve two masters." I always hated that saying,
partly because he would not tell us who the two masters
were. You were supposed to figure that out on your own.
Plus, I knew on a deep level that I was probably serving
the inferior master, and it was going to be major work to
switch masters. I now see who the two masters are, the
ego reality and the reality of the intuitive Spirit, God,
Universe, or Higher Self. These two realities are diametri-
cally opposed, total opposites. That was always hard to
get my head around, but I got it intuitively. For example,
you can't do "trust and faith" and "fear and doubt" at the
same time. That is the good news. There is no halfway
between the two realities; you are in one or the other.

Many of us try to operate with one foot in each reality.
But if you are feeling any hint of negativity, such as fear
or doubt or worry, you are in the ego reality. There is
no negativity in the Zone. Of course, you can have a

thoughtful concern if there is something to be avoided, but it won't have the negative quality of fear, doubt, or worry. Negative feelings are the result of negative visions of the future or negatively remembering the past. If you are in the Zone, the present moment, fear, doubt, and worry don't exist. Sometimes I feel the slightest hint of doubt or a vague fear of the future. I have learned that this is more of a mental habit than anything real, and I can switch it off. I simply notice that I am allowing some negative thoughts or feelings to enter my awareness, which is now a flashing red light that the ego is in the building, planting seeds of self-sabotage. I have to choose at that point which master I am going to serve (listen to).

Another common aspect of the ego combined with your analytical mind is that the ego thinks in terms of black or white, never gray. The answer to your challenge will be either intuitive OR analytical. It somehow doesn't occur to the ego that the best answer is both or some combination. I like to say that most often the best answer to a problem is some shade of gray. As I have mentioned, the analytical and the intuitive work best together as a team. They perform different necessary functions.

The ego relates to the physical body as who we are (five senses). The ego's concept of reality is that we have a body, and we are separate from everyone else because that is how it appears in physical reality. However, we are not limited to the ego's reality of being a separate physical body. We have other realities, such as being a spirit that is connected to other spirits and all other things in some way.

The problem is that because the ego only considers what can be perceived by the five senses as real, being intuitive is not a reliable source. However, the ego has to allow you to be intuitive because it is not in charge; you are. Your ego will make its best case to ignore the fleeting fancy of the unknown and go with what it calls the "real world" that you can see, hear, touch, taste, and smell. To the ego, anything else in your mind doesn't count.

The statement "Your ego is not in charge: you are" invites further discussion. Your level of awareness and personal development will determine how much you relate to yourself as your ego.

Many people don't see much more than their ego sees. We have been programmed to be egos for thousands of years. Therefore, your ego is a highly integrated part of you that can feel so familiar you may think that it is who you are. The reality is that you have the capacity to be much more if you learn to identify the ego's limited agenda and replace it with a more intelligent version of yourself.

The best evidence that you are not your ego is that you can choose to go against the ego's advice. If you can recognize that your ego is telling you to stop doing something that it thinks is potentially dangerous, you don't have to takes its advice. So, who is it saying no to the ego's warning? Who is making a decision to do something different than what the ego wants? It's like the old cartoons that show the devil on one shoulder whispering into one ear and an angel on the other shoulder whispering into the other ear. Most of the time, the selfish, controlling, calculating ego is going to sound more like the devil than the angel.

The most important thing to see at this point is that we have a reality that is created by the part of us we call the ego, and we can go against its advice if we want. The reason this is important is that if you can argue with your ego or go against its advice, you are not your ego. You are something bigger. I like to say that who we really are is the *chooser*.

You can choose the thoughts and feelings you want to have at any time, any place, regardless of the demands of the voices in your head. Certainly, there are many powerful, programmed responses that you have to contend with, and it can seem you don't have any choice. But who you really are has the potential to choose to think and feel whatever you want, as contrary as that may sound.

People who are not familiar with the idea that you are the chooser will argue that what you think and feel just happens, and you don't really have any choice about it. That is how it appears at first glance. It is a big step in awareness to see that you have more control over your thoughts and feelings than you may have ever considered. Becoming aware of our power to choose under any circumstances is extremely useful in our mission to free ourselves from the maniacal control of the ego.

I have a pet peeve that I want to mention here about the use of the word "mind." Many intelligent people use the terms "mind" and "ego" interchangeably, which to me is not accurate and ultimately confusing. The mind is a huge part of who we are and actually holds or hosts the chooser. Your mind can be an ego or your mind can be a Spirit. Your mind can be whatever you want it be. But you can't function in everyday life without a mind. With no mind, you are a vegetable, and you will need life support. The idea that you transcend your mind to be a spirit sounds good, but what really should be said is that you transcend your ego to become a spirit, not your mind. We need our minds to ignore the ego and choose a different path. We can't be in an enlightened state without the mind to hold it.

Experts refer to the conscious mind, the sub-conscious mind, the super-conscious mind, and other terms in an attempt to define consciousness. So yes, you can operate outside the "conscious mind," but you still need a mind to be able to function and know what level of awareness you are experiencing. In other words, if you somehow transcend the part of you that knows you exist, now you don't exist anymore, which gets way too confusing in a reality in which you need a body to play the game. Sounds like a fun conversation for a medical marijuana support group, but not a practical or functional solution for our purposes. So, gurus, my recommendation is that we don't use the words "mind" and "ego" interchangeably. Let's define the mind as our source of awareness or perception of Self (capitol "S") rather than a collection of ego-based behaviors or bad habits we are trying to give up (self with a small "s").

My greatest experience base of what you are up against as you start to ignore your ego and listen to your intuitive instincts in the Zone is making prospecting calls to promote yourself or a product/service. I realize that many of you reading this book don't have to make sales calls, but most of you have to promote yourself, so you will relate to the discussion either way. Most importantly, the same principles apply to any issue when it comes to tangling with the ego.

As I mentioned earlier, I have been coaching sales people with a specialty in the financial services business (investments and life insurance) most of my career. Prospecting is what we call putting yourself out there to have conversations with people about what you do or how you could help them. How the ego reacts to prospecting has given me a job for over thirty years. I have become an expert on teaching people how to prospect without the distractions of the ego, which, by the way, hates prospecting.

I have also used the act of prospecting in my own coaching practice as a way to train myself to stay in the intuitive Zone and ignore the ego. I make thousands of prospecting calls each year to practice staying in the Zone. Many people think that's a little nuts. But I can assure you it makes me a better coach than the people who attempt to deal with the issue of overcoming the fear of self-promotion with the ego's good ideas. Also, in the process of making all these prospecting calls for years, I have become highly skilled on the phone. Most of the people I call I have not met, yet they typically thank me for calling them, and many of them hire me to help them with a coaching project!

I would not recommend cold calling to my financial services clients for a variety of reasons. I say that because I don't want anyone to think I am an advocate of cold calling over the other more effective means of connecting with people today. And, I am quick to say that cold calling is not my favorite thing to do; however, it is a powerful way to train yourself to stay in the Zone. Going back to the football example, it's like learning to catch a football without being worried about the powerful athlete who's been professionally trained to physically hit you as hard as possible the second the ball is within your reach. Of course, making prospecting calls does not involve physical danger, but the ego would like you to think it does. The ego's reaction to any kind of potential discomfort is the same: Run, don't walk, in the opposite direction!

Let's make some prospecting calls together. Or, at least you can listen in to what goes on in my head as I make calls. I have hundreds of pre-qualified people to call. I find it helps to have a lot of people to call because if I let my ego get too involved in deciding who I am going to call, it slows the process down to a snail's pace, and I make far fewer calls. If I take an attitude of *just call people,* it doesn't matter who I call, I make a lot more calls.

Another effective approach: *Let's see how many people I can call in the next hour.* It keeps the ego from judging and evaluating everyone I am getting ready to call. I just look at the name on my computer screen and dial the number. As I have mentioned, the ego has no clue about who people are before I call them. But it will use its past experience to make up all kinds of information about who it thinks these people are. The ego can't prove that any of its made-up information is true. Most of the time, almost none of what the ego predicts turns out to be true. But the ego is a clever salesman and knows when you are vulnerable to its suggestions. The ego is deceptively cunning in this scenario, and you have to learn to recognize and ignore all the ego's strategies. If I let my ego decide who to call, the list would be shortened to sure bets with no risk. That would limit my calls to a couple a day, if that. Hard to make any money with those numbers.

As I dial the phone, I often keep a yellow pad to the right of my computer so I can make notes. This can be the key to having a successful phoning session. Usually, as I dial the phone, my ego starts in with things like, "Are you sure this is the best time to phone? It's pretty early. I think people would be more receptive after lunch, don't you?" Or "Are you sure these are the right people to be calling? They look awfully successful to me, which means they probably already have a coach or don't need one at this point." These are totally logical ploys by the ego to do one thing, get me to stop taking action that has an element of the unknown. The ego does not like the unknown and in particular does not like the unknown potential for rejection.

You have to become extremely sensitive to any negativity the ego can put forth. It is not unusual for me to have the thought that there has to be a better way to find clients. My ego loves to tell me that making prospecting calls is a waste of time. It is worth noting that I have spent thousands of hours doing every other type of prospecting and promotion you can imagine. I actually prefer the simplicity of making prospecting calls. Unfortunately, I know my ego is never going to agree. The ultimate negative judgement by the ego is that I am in the wrong job. This, of course, is ridiculous. I have spent more time than most creating an ideal career for myself. The point is that even with overwhelming evidence that says making calls is the best way for me to find new clients, my ego will never give up trying to talk me out of it!

So as the ego tries to come up with things that will stop me from making calls, I counter with all the tricks I have learned to take away the ego's power. Here are a few more favorites:

- "The only way you can fail at prospecting is not to make the effort." This one is so obvious it hurts to say it. What also hurts is all the time I have spent ignoring this fact. The reality is that if you make an effort with a sincere intent to help people, something good will come from it. The Universe is watching. I call it *mystical momentum*. This is pretty far out there for your average analytical type, but my coaching clients become believers. In other words, you can't prospect and not make any money (assuming you have a decent offer). The business you do may not actually come from the calls you make, but it will happen; this makes the analytical ego crazy. In fact, I would say that if you want to do more business, simply make more prospecting calls. It doesn't matter what happens on any of the calls. Just the mere act of making the calls sends out a message to the Universe that you want more business. And the Universe will respond. Of course, the ego lives in the "real world," where everything is based on provable cause and effect. So, the idea of mystical momentum is outrageous to the ego! This is one of those situations in which you have to realize you know better than your ego. If you consistently do anything with a positive intent, you will see positive results. There will be people who respond positively to your offer.

• "I don't have to sell anything; these are public relations calls. I am calling people to see how they are doing and if I can be of any help. It doesn't matter how they respond." This is a good one, because the ego is convinced if you are any good, everyone will say yes. So then when someone says no, which happens frequently, the ego then tells you that you must be doing something wrong, so you should take a time out and rethink what you are saying to people. Remember the goal of the ego is to get you to stop taking action that could create an unknown result, such as finding someone who wants and needs your help!

• "Don't allow any negative judgements about any aspect of prospecting." This is a major blow to the ego's power. If you stop negatively judging anything, you move into the Zone. Combine not negatively judging with maintaining the innocence of a child, and you are in a state of total trust and faith, symptoms of being in the Zone. That is the "I" (innocence) and the "N" (no negativity) of the PIN Formula. My experience is that if you shut down all negative judgement about whatever you are doing and maintain the innocence of a child in your interactions, you are automatically in the present moment, which is the "P" part of the PIN formula.

Let's say a receptionist gives me a hard time. I used to be frustrated with being asked, "Who are you with?" I have considered saying, "Actually, I am alone at the moment. Is there something you want to tell me?" It will feel good to your ego to say something clever or confronting to get back at people for making it hard for you to get through to the boss. I used to fight back and try to challenge the receptionist. I might say things like, "Are you sure you want to be making that decision for your boss? Maybe you should put me through so he can decide for himself." It sounds logical enough but rarely works. The problem with such responses is that they are ego based, which means the goal is dominance and control. Most receptionists are going to unconsciously resist that energy.

Most important is to commit to *no negativity*, which means I can't get upset with the receptionist no matter how rude or difficult she (sometimes he) is. I have found it works much better just to say why I am calling and not try to outsmart the receptionist. The first time I did this I was amazed. I thought to myself, "It can't be that easy." Certainly, operating from a state of innocence does not guarantee a change in rude or judgemental people, but my results show that I get through to twice as many people with the innocent approach. Also, I have found that if I don't get along with the receptionist, I usually don't do well with the owner anyway. If I feel any negative energy coming from the receptionist, I politely and quickly get off the call. This, of course, drives my ego crazy because it wants proof that the owner is as negative as the receptionist. My intuition knows better.

- This brings to mind one of the most powerful ego stoppers, "My job is not to sell people, but to find the people God wants me to help." This is a powerful focus because it easily trumps anything the ego can come up with. When you are in the Zone, there is only abundance, so there is no shortage of prospects, clients, money, or anything else you could want. This is an unreasonable state of mind to the ego, which is obsessed with surviving in a world of scarcity. So, to discard a sales lead because you don't like his or her receptionist is a major demonstration of trust and faith. Your ego will call that an act of stupidity. You never know who is going to buy and who isn't. That is true, but when I'm in the Zone, I have no time for negativity, especially not from the people I am calling!

If you feel negativity, the most powerful thing to do is move on to the next call. You get a rush of energy every time you choose abundance over scarcity; expect your ego to be rolling its eyes at your foolishness.

If you are interested in learning more about how to overcome your resistance to self-promotion, I put thirty years of research into my recent book, *How I Conquered Call Reluctance, Fear of Self-Promotion & Increased My Prospecting!* It is available in soft cover, Kindle, and audio through Amazon.

One final thought on making prospecting calls (or doing anything challenging) involves how you react when you succeed. You would think that the obvious response to finding someone interested in what you are offering would be reason to pause and have a party. The downside of getting too elated about something good happening is that it creates a strong contrast to the calls that are not so good, which actually creates a negative. I mentioned earlier that I like to acknowledge the moment and let some of my elated energy come out in whatever way seems appropriate at the time. After my brief expression of triumph, I calm myself down to a more Zen approach of seeing all the calls I make as important. Because, remember, it doesn't matter what happens on any one call. The fact that you are taking action (making calls) is more important than anything else. Action with a positive intent will create some positive results, often in ways you will never understand. The analytical ego is judging and evaluating every call telling you what you did wrong and what you could have done. The intuitive Spirit knows that God will provide if you make an effort.

Opportunities to use the PIN Formula are happening all the time. Every time your comfort zone is challenged or when what you expect or what you hope will happen does not happen, you have a choice to make about how you respond. Are you going to listen to the voice of the ego or the intuitive Spirit? I lived in Southern California for twenty years. It is a common experience to be driving along at high speed making great time to your destination and then be confronted with having to come to a complete stop on an expressway packed with cars as far as you can see. Do you then listen to your ego and all its negative chatter, or do you use the time to find a more quiet and pleasant place to be and reflect?

We are programmed by the ego to want what we want when we want it, like a spoiled little kid. One of my more colorful mentors used to call the inner child *the inner brat.* The ego feels justified in being upset that the Universe is not giving it what it wants and doing it right now! The ego will go on and on with its critical judgements and explanations about why so many people don't see the great wisdom of your ego and all of its award-winning answers to the world's problems. It can even feel good to indulge your anger or frustration at a world that is not giving you what you want, but in the end, this approach has to backfire. Any approach to solving problems with a negative element is going to create a leak in the boat. Sure, you can push for an immediate solution to your problem, but if there is any hint of negativity in your approach, that won't be the end of the problem.

There is a profound difference between the solutions your controlling ego gives you and the solutions coming from your intuitive Spirit or Higher Self. The ego's answers, because they include an aspect of negativity, will cause another problem either now or later. The answers coming from your intuition don't have that negative aspect. If you are operating in the Zone, there is no negativity. My experience is that my intuitive solutions tend not to create more problems in the same way the ego's solutions do. You will have to test this theory for yourself. This is part of the value of keeping a log of what happens when you take action on your intuitive directives. You will see if the problem persists in some way or if it goes away altogether. My records reflect with great consistency that your intuitive Higher Self is brilliant at making problems totally disappear if you keep being intuitive!

There is a big difference between being an ego and being an intuitive Spirit. You have to decide which reality you want to live in. In the world of the intuitive Spirit, you live in a reality of peace, love, joy, and abundance with no opposite. Or you can live the "normal" life of an ego, which includes varying levels of success but always accompanied with some fear, suffering, misfortune, and a propensity for being treated unfairly, just to name a few of the big negatives. Most people choose the ego reality because it's familiar, it is seemingly what everyone is doing, and it offers the illusion of more control. We are programmed from birth to choose the ego reality. Meanwhile, the thrill and ecstasy of the Zone reality of the Higher Self is sitting there waiting for us to wake up and embrace our true inheritance.

The most important thing to do now is to experiment. Don't just take my word for it. Find your own truth and decide for yourself!

Following is a table I created to show the basic qualities of the ego versus the intuitive Spirit:

EGO (false self—created by other people's opinions of you.)	SPIRIT (real self—accessed from within, from your intuition, conscience, and soul.)
• Has an illusion of separation from Source.	• One with the Source/God/Universe.
• Created from birth forward by what you perceive others think of you.	• You are born with your Spirit Self intact. It is complete and ready for a new life.
• Focused on survival and the assurance of survival.	• Focused on fulfilling its visions, purpose, mission, calling.
• Has a fear you might not survive.	• Doesn't think negative thoughts.
• Lives in the past and the future.	• Lives in the present moment.
• Data is based on past experience.	• Data source immeasurable, total recall.
• Likes status quo/comfort zone, resistant to change, innovation, and creativity.	• Confident in ability to adapt and find workable solutions to any challenge.
• Looks for what is wrong and what could go wrong.	• Assumes you will be shown how to succeed in any situation.
• Constantly judging and evaluating.	• Listens for what feels intuitively right.
• External focus for information.	• Internal focus for information.
• Controlling; needs to be right about the information it has collected or believes.	• Flowing; looks for what feels intuitively right, or what works with good for all.
• Tries to protect you from what is happening or could happen.	• Focused on responding appropriately in the present moment.
• Tries to avoid mistakes.	• Sees mistakes as required to succeed.
• Sees a scarcity of resources.	• Sees an abundance of resources.
• Gets analytical under pressure, wants observable proof before taking action.	• Trusts life's process. Trusts that an answer or solution will appear as needed.
• Trusts observable proof and the five physical senses.	• Intuition trumps intellect for direction and timing. Recognizes unseen influences.
• Exclusive: "You OR me..."	• Inclusive: "You AND me..."
• Limited creativity within a framework.	• Unlimited imagination and creativity.
• Scared, fearful, cautious.	• Fearless, undaunted, unstoppable.
• Fun is coasting, being entertained.	• Fun is challenge, innocent pleasures.

5

Trim Tabs

I LIKE THE IDEA OF A TRIM TAB *because it's a little thing that can make big things happen.* For example, on an ocean liner, the rudder is massive. Rather than put all the pressure on one steering mechanism to turn the big rudder, little rudders (trim tabs) are used. A trim tab is a little rudder on the big rudder that gets the water moving in the direction the captain wants to turn the boat. Trim tabs help turn the big rudder with just the forward movement of the boat through the water. This takes great pressure off of the steering mechanism.

Similarly and more familiar are the flaps on an airplane, which are trim tabs in addition to the rudder. You adjust the flap, and the air hitting the flap changes the direction or speed of the plane. You have probably seen a movie where a flight attendant (not a pilot) is trying to land the jet. As they read the manual on how to land the plane, at some point there will be an instruction for "full flaps." The flaps then act like breaks to slow the plane down both in the air and after the plane has touched down.

There are many examples of this technology. The idea is to use something small to make something much bigger happen. For our purposes, the rest of this chapter will be shorter thoughts (trim tabs) using different words to help increase your ability to get in the Zone and stay in the Zone. I have purposely minimized graphics so you can decide for yourself what is important to you.

I could probably write a book on any one of these trim tabs. So, this is an attempt to keep this book shorter and easier to get through. This chapter will help you rethink some of what you would call "normal." Have fun with these ideas. Remember the goal is to help you be in the Zone, ignore the ego reality, and do what feels intuitively right to you.

Here we go…

1. The original reality we were given was one of peace, love, joy, and abundance with no opposite. In other words, no negativity or suffering; those are actually human creations or aberrations of the raw material we were originally given.

2. There are two opposing thought systems. The ego reality is based on fear, control, survival, and constant critical judgement of what you are doing based on a collection of life experiences fraught with misperception due to a narrow focus of reality. The Spirit-based reality is sourced by love, no negativity, living in the present moment with the innocence of a child, and following your Higher Self through intuitive guidance, which leads to the perception of truth and the experience of miracles (things falling into place in both logical and unexpected ways).

3. At some point in ancient history, we learned to negativity judge the original reality we were given, which

had no negativity. This is the source of all the negative things in life and the subsequent suffering they create. The good news is that we were also given free will, which means we can give up our addiction to negativity and the endless suffering that it brings. This is not easy. We have been programmed to choose the ego reality for thousands of years.

4. The ego is brilliant at disguising itself as you or who you think you are. It claims to be our protector in a dangerous world full of negative consequences actually created by the ego. The ego causes us to be obsessed with our own survival and blame others for whatever bad things have happened. The ego is also obsessed with its own survival. It doesn't want you to figure out that it is the cause of all negativity and that it really doesn't have answers to your problems, only guesses. Your ego is not your friend, but it wants you to think that it is.

5. Jesus is to have said, "If you have faith as small as a mustard seed, you can say to this mountain, move from here to there, and it will move. Nothing will be impossible for you." A small amount of faith is extremely powerful. Also, from my own experience, a mustard seed of doubt can destroy your dreams. Therefore, a small amount of faith while not allowing a speck of doubt will make you a powerhouse.

6. In a world with no negativity, there is nothing wrong with you. You are perfect the way you are. There is nothing to fix. This doesn't mean that we have not felt the effects of negativity in this lifetime. However, you can begin to minimize the effects of negativity if you learn to live in the Zone.

7. In the Zone, you can't fail at any meaningful endeavor. This does not mean everything you attempt is

going to work the first time. But there is no devastating
failure. You learn to succeed by letting life and your results
teach you. But you must be open to the truth of the intuitive Spirit as opposed to the dogma of misguided beliefs
presented by the ego. We learn to succeed at whatever we
attempt through a series of trial and correction or trial and
adaptation. Anything else would be too boring.

8. You are not your ego; you are the chooser. The proof
that you are not your ego is that you can go against its
advice. People who are not familiar with the idea that you
are the chooser will argue that what you think and feel just
happens, and you don't really have any choice about it. That
is how it appears at first glance. It is a big step in awareness
to realize that you have more control than you may have
ever realized, and this is extremely useful in our mission
to free ourselves from the maniacal control of the ego.

9. Almost no real change from what has happened
in the past is possible until you see the ego as the enemy.
Until you understand how the ego works, you are at the
affect of the ego and the rules of its negative reality.

The goal of the ego is to keep us asleep and unaware
of the power we have to create. We were originally given
a reality of unlimited possibilities. This is a far cry from
the world the ego would have us live in. The illusion the
ego offers is one of hope, but the harsh reality is one of
resistance to change.

10. The ego has created a world full of problems that
it can't solve and wants us to think that is has the answers. As Nouk Sanchez puts it, the mantra of the ego is
"Seek and do not find." Unbelievable that we seek guidance from a source that has promised protection but has
no intention or ability of giving us an answer that will
make any real difference.

11. The potential for subtle self-sabotage just big enough to keep you generally where you are in life is way more likely than getting a breakthrough to new behavior. I have experienced slow growth and many breakthroughs in my life, but nothing like what happens when you start to learn how to ignore the ego and its insidious agenda.

12. Until you can hold the PIN Formula, real and lasting change is possible but unlikely.

13. Learning to ignore the ego so you can get in the Zone is a skill. Possibly the most important skill you will ever learn for a better life.

14. It takes guts and practice to confront the conventional wisdom of the world created by the ego. Expect resistance, your own and from other people. The ego is formidable and relentless. The ego knows every trick in the book and it doesn't sleep. But there is one tactic for which the ego has no defense: If you ignore the ego in your own awareness, it has no power!

15. Albert Einstein said, "We can't solve problems by using the same kind of thinking we used when we created them." The variation I like is "You can't solve the problem in the same paradigm that created the problem." This is a consistent trick of the ego. It will have you seeking answers to the problem without shifting to a perspective big enough to solve the problem. The net effect is no real change. The problem will persist or live in another form, or the solution to the problem creates more problems—all of which are examples of ego genius designed to keep us asleep and stuck.

16. There is the popular phrase, "You have to get out of your own way." This is true, and what is actually being said is that you have to learn to ignore the negativity,

doubt, and resistance created by the ego in order to make any real progress. We are in our own way most of the time if we are listening to the ego. The ego has a collection of beliefs based on its limited perspective about how life works in physical reality that holds us back from what we could easily accomplish without this distraction.

17. If you notice negative thoughts and feelings, stop affirming the negativity by using the word "I." Instead of saying, "I am afraid of the future." Experiment with, "My ego is afraid of the future. As an intuitive Spirit, I have no reason to be afraid." This takes some practice, but the idea is powerful. We have so absorbed the ego into our reality, we think we are the ones being negative. Being negative in any way requires a choice even though you may not be aware that you have made one. You can choose not to be negative. Thinking negative thoughts or having negative feelings is not a law of the Universe, like gravity. You have the power to choose differently, always did, always will. And yes, some negative thoughts and feelings are going to require more energy to let go of than others.

18. The ego relates to the physical body as who we are. The ego's concept of reality is that we have a body, and we are separate from everyone else because that is how it appears in physical reality. Everyone has his or her own body. However, we are not limited to the ego's reality of being a separate physical body. We have access to other realities, such as that of being a spirit that is connected to other spirits or nature in ways we cannot explain.

19. Functionally, the ego cannot discern truth. That is a skill reserved for the intuitive Spirit. The ego can only judge whether the information being presented matches or does not match the information it has collected. The intuition of Higher Intelligence, or Spirit is not available to

the ego. A good thief or a con man has intuitive instincts, but since the intent is negative, there will be a price to pay at some point. A negative intent has to manifest a negative result eventually. And the negative result may have little to do with the original negative act. Negativity often manifests itself in health issues, broken relationships, and money problems, to name a few of the big ones.

20. Simplify your life as much as possible. The ego loves to keep us so busy we don't have time to think and reflect. Life seems to get busier and busier as we constantly chase things we think we need to be happy. Much of our "hamster on the treadmill" existence is encouraged by an ego that has no clue what will make us happy. Also, from an ego perspective, no matter what we achieve, there is always something missing. Guess what's missing?

21. I am sure there is a Biblical quote for everything I have said in this book. But the still, small voice tells me that book learning is not as powerful as having an alive, in-the-present-moment relationship with your intuitive Spirit. Therefore, information about things is less important than developing the trust and faith to listen to your intuitive Spirit and follow its guidance. Knowing all the "dos and don'ts" and all the rules is never going to be as powerful as asking your intuitive Spirit for guidance and waiting for the answer. *This also requires faith, which requires guts.* There is nothing wrong with knowing the dos and don'ts and all the rules; just don't place them above your intuitive knowing. You are looking for the *particularly appropriate response* from your Higher Self.

22. The world needs to be shown the possibilities, not just new versions of the same old thing. The ego's goal is to keep us asleep and resist change. We need more brave people to see options beyond the ego reality. In a world

controlled by egos, we will not see what is possible, or we won't believe what is possible. We need to question conventional wisdom and be willing to experiment with what feels intuitively right.

23. Regular miracles are one of the incentives for being an intuitive Spirit living in the Zone. This is a powerful incentive, but most of us have been programmed to see miracles as luck or flukes. Keep a log of the miracles you experience as you spend more time in the Zone. A pattern will emerge that your ego does not want you to see. Your ego will actually try to get you to forget about your miracles as fast as they happen!

24. Everything I have presented in this book is common sense to some, which is interestingly also uncommon. The ego has its own brand of common sense that is not common sense but rather the misguided conclusions of a large number of egos. Common sense needs to be based on what feels intuitively right, not on a collection of made-up rules about how life works. Of course, some of those ego-based rules are going to include elements of truth, but a rule without the interpretation of the intuitive Spirit is going to cause disappointments.

25. In the simple and powerful words of my spiritual mentor, "Think good thoughts."

26. You will begin to realize that ego programming is holding you back in hundreds of ways, many of which you were not even aware of. Herein lies the seed of rebellion and inspiration to discover who you really are without the ego's baggage. Who would you be and what would you be capable of with nothing slowing you down or distracting you from what you came to do? The only way to get a real answer to this question is to learn to ignore the ego!

27. Being solution-oriented is an excellent way to describe maintaining a Spirit-based approach. In the Zone, a solution will appear. At the monastery, one of the teachings was "You will get what you need as you need it." This of course, like all sayings, has much more power if you are living in the Zone, or you are putting the Spirit first. To be committed to figuring out a solution to whatever challenges you face sounds good, but it is not as powerful or as effective as being willing to ask a question of your Higher Self and wait for the answer. Some might call that prayer. As an intuitive Spirit, you will be given an answer on what to do next if you open yourself up. As an ego, your answer will be based on conventional wisdom or your own past experience and will usually include a hint of fear, doubt, or worry. It won't be a peaceful answer because your ego is guessing. Would you rather be a force of nature or someone hoping they know what they are doing?

28. Attitude and holding a positive vision are highly related. What do you see in the future? What do you expect? With the ego, you have to work at maintaining a positive vision due to a propensity to be looking for what could go wrong and trying to avoid it. As an intuitive Spirit, you expect things to work out. And you may not be particularly concerned about how things will work, you just know they will. If you're in the Zone, where you can't fail and you are backed by the Universe, there is no reason to expect anything but success!

29. There is always a moment of truth when you are faced with another obstacle or setback. How are you going to respond? Sometimes you have worked hard, you are exhausted, and the bad news catches you off guard. You respond negatively. So far, not a problem.

The trick is to quickly get back to a state of mind in which you can best deal with the issue objectively without the negativity—and maybe even see if there is a lesson that can be learned.

30. Critically judging anything will tend to distract you from learning what there is to learn from your experience or your results. Negative judgements will also keep you from taking the risks you need to take to do the required activities for your vision to manifest. Your ego will resist doing the required activities because if you forge ahead, you will succeed at a new level, and that will create change, and the ego hates change. Some call this fear of success, which is really just fear of change. If there is fear involved, it's coming from the ego.

31. Present all challenges, obstacles, and problems to the intuitive Spirit to resolve in the best possible way. The ego is not going to find a way out. The ego's goal is no real change or creation of more problems.

32. Other egos will be critical of you. That is what egos do. They judge and complain because whatever is wrong or not working must be your fault, not theirs, especially if you challenge the ego database of how life works by being unpredictable or unconventional. You are challenging ego norms, which I totally endorse as long as the intent is positive for all concerned.

33. The ego version of repentance is to feel bad about your mistakes, your failures, and your transgressions. Other terms synonymous with feeling bad are "feel remorse," "regret," "be sorry," "rue," "reproach oneself," and "be ashamed."

Imagine a reality with no negativity. What does "repent" mean in such a world? The dictionary does a great job here:

REPENTANCE, a transliteration of the Greek
word metanoia, can be defined as "a transforma-
tive change of heart; or a spiritual conversion."
The term suggests repudiation, change of mind,
repentance, and atonement; but "conversion" and
"reformation" may best approximate its connota-
tion. The repentance called for throughout the
Bible is a summons to a personal, absolute and
ultimate unconditional surrender to God. In
repenting, one makes a complete change of
direction (180° turn) toward God.

Could repentance be a commitment to living in the
Zone and ignoring the ego?

34. I like formulas and have created one to remind me
of the importance of doing the required activities toward
any vision" RAN2. This stands for *Do the Required Activities
Intuitively.* N2 is my abbreviation for intuitive or intuitively.

Putting the formulas from this book together looks
like:

VAA / PIN / RAN2

Vision, Action, Attitude; Present Moment, Innocence,
No Negativity; Do the Required Activities Intuitively.

35. What if praising God is more about being and
doing than thinking about it? What if the greatest gift
you can give to God and to the world, the thing you
actually came to do, is to live in the present moment with
the innocence of a child and ignore the negative ego?

36. A thought-provoking side note, something I have
noticed with consistency, is that taking action makes you
smarter. Something happens when you jump into the fray.

Your mind wakes up, your body wakes up, the juices start to flow, and all of a sudden you have access to parts of your brain that were not there a second ago.

37. Being in the Zone automatically aligns your will with God's Will. Whatever happens while you are in the Zone is what God wants to happen somehow. We may not understand exactly how it works, but that is the way it was designed. The problem is that most of us don't spend much time in the Zone, so the impact of our results becomes muddled and confused. If everyone were operating in the Zone most of the time, the world would quickly become everything we hoped was possible, and the negatives would disappear. Sounds like science fiction, but we are powerful enough to create such a place if enough of us want to do it. It all starts with you and me.

The concept of aligning your will with God's Will is so important, let me say it another way: Aligning yourself with what feels intuitively right is aligning yourself with God's Will. *Life on Earth was designed to have the thing that feels intuitively right to be what God wants to happen.*

38. The intuitive Spirit is fearless, dauntless, unstoppable, and loaded with loving kindness. What is there to be afraid of in a world with no negatives? It's hard for us to imagine, but that world exists, and you have the power to live in it. Of course, there is a transition process away from the ego reality, but God's Loving Reality is here for us, and it is just as real as the physical version of the world created by the ego.

The cheering squad on the side of the Spirit reality is way bigger. All the Spirits that are not physically in this reality are cheering for you to wake up from the ego's insane reality. They are hoping some of us will figure this out and free us all!

39. Some say our greatest fear is God's Love. That has never felt right to me. I understand the idea, and it makes me stop and think. But based on what I know to be true, if you are being an intuitive Spirit, there is no fear, which means there can be no fear of God's love in the Zone. My conclusion is that we only fear God's love as an ego.

40. Reread your favorite parts of this book. There is a saying that you can't step in a moving river in the same place twice. When you reread a book, you will be in a different place. Your ego will argue that you have already read this book so there is no point in reading it again. What the ego does not understand is that if you read it again, you will get many new insights. There are several books that I read every year or so because they are reaffirming, and I always get something new that is well worth the effort. Rereading a book you like can be much more impactful than reading every book on a subject. Making the change to living in the Zone is not determined by how much information you have about it. It's about making a leap of faith and doing it.

41. We have been programmed by the ego to not hear what is presented in this book or at least to disregard it. So don't be surprised if you have a good feeling about a concept or idea but also find that you have difficulty remembering it. That is one of the reasons I wrote this book. You need a source to go back to and say, "Now what was that idea that I liked so much that seems to be hard to hang onto?" Because of this phenomenon, you need to make your own notes and reread them regularly until the Zone becomes your chosen reality without thinking.

42. The ego would have you think that enlightenment is something that would take many years of process and study and even then only be available to a few. The reality is that you open the door to enlightenment the second you ignore the ego and get into the Zone. At that moment, you are living in the original reality we were given in which we are naturally enlightened. Also, when you move into the Zone, you are instantly Spirit. Incredibly, being a spirit is not something you need to learn how to do. It is who you already are when you ignore the ego.

43. Enlightenment has been described to me by people I respect as the reversal of all worldly thoughts and beliefs, all created by the ego. I would like to add to this equation that you can exponentially speed up this process by learning to ignore the ego and live in the Zone. The ego does not want you to know that you have that kind of power. The ego is obsessed with its own survival in addition to making you think it is in charge of your survival. And it's been at it for thousands of years. You can expect major resistance to the idea of enlightenment. It doesn't even occur to most people that this is something we should be working toward, thanks to the ego.

44. In a world created by egos, there is a never-ending competition for scarce resources. This is an illusion, of course, but it appears to be real in the physical world. The real competition is not with other people but with the ego and its hold on you. Once you learn to ignore the ego's obsession with dominance and control in order to survive in a negative world, you have no competition. There is only abundance of whatever you need. A challenging thought worth considering. You could say the ultimate competition is to ignore the ego and stay in the Zone. You are unstoppable there and a force of nature. Your word becomes law in the Universe. Doesn't that sound better than fear, doubt, worry, and suffering?

45. Paul Zane Pilsner, a professor at Columbia University, wrote a book called, *God Wants You to Be Rich.* This is not a religious book in the usual sense. One of his main points is how to deal with the idea of scarcity. He eloquently makes the case, with great examples, that rather than be afraid of running out of something such as fossil fuel, it would be better to just run out. Because we live in an underlying reality of abundance, even though the ego would vehemently disagree, we will never run out of what we need from a bigger perspective. If we run out of something such as fossil fuel, a replacement will appear almost instantly. And there will always be people working on the replacement long before we run out. In the case of fossil fuel, viable alternatives have existed for decades. But the egos at the corporations do not want anyone to know that and will put titanic energy into keeping those alternatives from being seriously considered. Of course, if the egos at the fossil fuel corporations can control the profits of the replacement energy, they are more open to considering other options.

46. Some challenging thoughts that need to be considered: What if the human body were designed to renew itself indefinitely? What if there were no death before the ego was created? Aging, debilitating disease, fatal accidents, and death are negative events. In the original reality, there was no negativity. What if the ego made up the story that Heaven is a place you go when you die to have a better life? What if the ego wants us to justify a life of suffering by being able to go to Heaven for our reward? But what if Heaven is only a way station until you can get a new body to come back to Earth and try again?

What if we were given Heaven here on Earth to live in, and we scorched it with negativity and subsequent suffering. What if this reality used to be Heaven before we learned the ways of the ego and turned it into Heaven AND Hell?

The good news is that if we chose to add Hell to Heaven, we can choose to make it just Heaven again. If this world were originally Heaven, doesn't it make sense to try to get that back? I know it sounds like an impossible task, but it's not as hard as it sounds. Be assured, the ego is going to make it appear inconceivable. But the reality is that it's not that complicated. As I have previously stated, it is actually relatively simple, but it does take guts. It requires the ability to access your intuition and then take the leap of faith to act on your intuitive instincts. Most of us need help with this, but this is not an impossible task. Many of us use our intuitive skills every day. We have just not had the proper focus of creating without the restrictions of the ego.

47. Remember the Michael Jackson song *Man in the Mirror?* He memorialized in song the idea that if you want to change the world, you have to start with yourself. You start with your life first. You don't have to worry about anyone else. *You* must learn how to ignore the ego and live in the Zone. That is the single most powerful thing you can do to create real change. And that is how we transform the world, one human being at a time. And we have to focus on the people who are interested in making this change. Trying to talk dedicated egos into not being egos anymore is not a good use of our precious time and energy. Those folks will come around later, after enough of us have chosen to make the leap. We need to show them it works, and it's a better approach to life on Earth.

We can do this. We can support each other by sharing our insights and triumphs. We can encourage those who are ready for a transformation by spreading the word about what is possible. Ask your intuitive Spirit for direction on what you are supposed to do. Patiently and openly, listen for that guidance because it will come to you. There is a Divine promise, *"Ask, and it shall be given; seek, and ye shall find; knock, and the door shall be opened unto you."* (Luke). Biblical sayings take on new meaning when you live in the Zone. They become law in your universe rather than merely comforting ideas that you hope are true.

48. I have quoted Nouk Sanchez (*Take Me to Truth, The End of Death*) in this book a couple of times in short phrases. She deserves much more credit. The impact of her writing was nothing short of miraculous for me. She gave me key pieces of the puzzle to a lifelong search that opened the way to my most profound and powerful breakthroughs. Here is a summary from Nouk on our mission, should you choose to join the cause:

> As long as we choose to harbor the unconscious guilt [of the separated ego], keeping it safe in the dark, never daring to look at it, we will continue to find the source of our suffering in others, in the past, in situations, and in our bodies. When we finally decide we have had enough of the ego's frantically fruitless external search for the causes of both suffering and salvation, only then are we ready to start the journey of undoing the ego.

49. Every organization I have ever belonged to wanted me to find more members. This club is no exception. The difference here is that being a member can make your life better immediately and ultimately make the world a better place more quickly than anything that has ever been done. It all starts with you and me sharing our truth to those we think are ready for membership in the Zone.

I often hear people say, "I'm ok with everything you have said so far." I think many times people are pleasantly shocked at what I will bring up in an initial conversation. But my experience is that the right people are ready and seeking answers. Those are your best candidates, by the way, the truth seekers who I like to refer to as personal-growth junkies. They have always been a relatively small group, but that is changing.

In the monastery, they said that getting one person to God was worth a thousand hours of service. Getting people (strangers) to the monastery was one of the most challenging things I have ever done. But I did it many times, and some of those folks are still there. The good news with getting people into a discussion about being in the Zone is that it's much easier. There is alot of baggage and resistance to the God conversation. When you speak of spending more time in the Zone, the right people will say, "Tell me more."

When I had the idea for this book, I thought to myself, "I am going to write a book about how not to be an ego and promote it to a world full of egos." Who's going to buy the book? Obviously, it felt intuitively right, so here we are.

What is amazing and encouraging is how quickly the right people get this information. It's like lighting a match to newspaper for those who are ready. Keep that in mind if you are considering spreading the word. Don't worry about the ones who don't get it right away. They are not pioneers like you and me. And when you find a kindred spirit, you will be moved and inspired by the connection you feel, and that makes it all worthwhile.

50. You can teach what is presented in this book. Practice the PIN Formula and see how that works for you in your own life. You will make your own modifications; that is expected. Then teach from your own experience. That's what I'm doing. Teach people the PIN formula and see how they react. You can decide what to do from there. Maybe you know of a good book on the subject that you could recommend! There will be many more books on this topic in the near future, and I don't mean just from me. I will continue to write about what I learn from my coaching practice as I always have. What I predict is that as more people discover the power of ignoring the ego and living in the Zone, there will be many more books on this topic, which is a good thing. We need to get as many people as possible living in the Zone.

51. What are truth seekers looking for? Experiencing love is a great joy. We want to find love and give love in as many ways as we can. It is a great joy to experience being in the Zone. It is a place where there is no fear, no worry, no doubt, and no judging, just being and doing something you enjoy. For most, being in the Zone is a fleeting experience that happens a few times in a lifetime if they are lucky. People want more of the Zone.

We want peace of mind. We are hoping that our endeavors bring us peace. Unfortunately, living in the ego reality, we end up feeling that something is missing regardless of what we achieve. In contrast, the focus of the intuitive Spirit is to serve others rather than to focus selfishly only on getting for yourself. There is nothing wrong with having money; abundance is the natural state in the Zone. But being in the Zone is not about having abundance for just yourself or a select few. As a Spirit, you have a desire to create abundance for all the lives you touch. You want to serve others by your work, to make their lives better. You enjoy helping someone for no reason other than it feels right. You could say truth seekers are motivated by love, being in the Zone, peace of mind, giving, being of service, making a difference, and making the world a better place. All of these wonderful things we long for are available in the Zone, right here, right now!

52. The pull toward God, Spirit, Higher Power, Higher Self, Higher Intelligence, Universe, or whatever name you prefer is strong for those who are still aware enough to feel it. Unfortunately, many have been so taken over by the ego they have blocked out any awareness of the Spirit.

53. God is sending a subliminal message 24/7 that you can hear much better when you choose to live in the Zone. The message is, "I love you. Come home." Come home means to choose to live in the reality we were originally given that is based on love instead of fear—a reality of peace, love, joy, and abundance with no opposite. I can't speak for you, but that feels like home to me.

54. Let me close this chapter on trim tabs with a thought from Osho, a contemporary Indian guru who died in 1990. He was a character and fun to listen to. I have listened to many of the audio recordings of his teachings on my daily walks. I think he would like this book. One of the things he said that deeply touched me—and I am paraphrasing from memory—was "Some say God is love. I like to say, love IS God."

Epilogue

H ERE IS ONE MORE OF MY FAVORITE THINGS TO PONDER, which is a good way to send you back out into the adventure of life. Jesus said two things that stand out related to our discussion. I am relating the essence of what I heard, not a direct quote. One, he said, *anyone can do what I do, and you can do it better.* Two, *I only do what the Father tells me to do.* If you put those two thoughts together, there are some interesting possibilities. If anyone has the capacity to do the miracles that Jesus did, that ability has to be within our reach somehow. He didn't say only highly evolved beings after years of study can do what I do, He said *anyone can do it.* Stated differently, enlightenment is not a hidden secret that will take years, or some say lifetimes, to learn. It is available right now if you can learn to see the path that is being covered up by your ego programming.

The second part, *I only do what the Father tells me to do,* can only be one thing if you consider our options. Generally speaking, we can be analytical, emotional, intuitive, or some combination. I don't think the Father is going to speak through the analytical or emotional, which are both so tangled up with the ego. My intuitive sense is that that Father is going to speak through intuition, which the ego cannot control. Meditate on this. Remember we have been programmed to not listen to our intuition by the ego. I am not saying that all intuitive promptings are Divine guidance, but some of them have to be. My conclusion is that following our intuitive instincts is far more important than we ever imagined, and the ego does not want us to know that!

I invite you to join the adventure of living in the Zone as an intuitive Spirit. As one of my spiritual mentors, who was fond of using Hollywood references, would say, "This is a big movie and everyone has a part to play." The key question is "Are you going to play the inspired part given to you by God or the part your ego made up for you to maintain the status quo?" Let the games begin!

Appendices

VISION–CREATING QUESTIONS

FAVORITE RESOURCES

BIOGRAPHY

OPT IN TO MAILING LIST

OTHER BOOKS BY SIDNEY C. WALKER

HIRE SID AS YOUR COACH

VISION-CREATING QUESTIONS

A LOT OF THINGS IN LIFE APPEAR TO BE totally out of our control. However, we seem to have a say about some of the things that happen in our lives because of our creative ability. Quantum scientists keep uncovering new versions of this theme. Some say our creative ability is far more powerful than we ever imagined.

Two fascinating concepts from quantum physics stand out: One, solid matter is not really solid but mostly space and energy. Could that be a form of intention? Two, at the smallest possible level that we can see, what we see changes depending on who is looking at it. In other words, what you think you see is what gets created! I wonder how much of that we are doing.

However it works, a great way to jumpstart the creative process is to ask yourself a question, then see what pops into your mind. Or go deeper and ask yourself, "What do I really want to create?" then ask, "Of all those things I have listed, which ones feel intuitively right to me?" Then, "Which one do I start with?"

Here is a list of questions to get you started. The real list is endless.

What do I want to see?
What do I want to feel?
What do I want to experience?
What do I want to experience once?

What do I want to experience more than once?

What do I want to experience on a regular basis?

What do I want to touch?

What do I want to taste?

What do I want to smell?

What do I want to witness?

What do I want to do?

What do I want to master?

What do I want to be good at?

What do I want to learn?

What do I want to study?

What do I want to maintain?

What do I want to grow?

What do I want to stop doing?

What do I want to enhance in my life?

What do I want more of?

What do I want less of?

What do I want to get rid of?

What do I want to give up?

What do I want to add to my life?

Who do I want to add to my life?

What do I want that I don't have?

What would make me happy?

What would empower me?

What would be an outrageous goal for me
that somehow feels right?

What do I really want to feel, and what do I need
to do to feel that?

Write down the answers and any other questions that popped into your head as you read this list. Those are usually important clues.

FAVORITE RESOURCES

Books by Paramahansa Yogananda (Yogananda-SRF.org):
A favorite spiritual author and meditation resource,
brilliantly clear and understandable. Many practical
books, booklets, and audio on how to live life to its
fullest. Self- Realization Fellowship is the organization
in the U.S.

Books by Nouk Sanchez: A new author in my library
over the last couple of years. Nouk has studied *The
Course in Miracles* for over twenty years and is now
writing books on her discovery of being able to interpret
the advanced teachings of Jesus. A brilliant, clear voice
of truth. I highly recommend her books: *Take Me to Truth*
and *The End of Death*.

Books by Eric Butterworth: In the *Flow of Life* and *Spiritual
Economics*. A revered author in my library. Eric was a Unity
minister in Detroit who had thousands attending his service
every Sunday. A master of "staying in the flow," backing it
all up with scripture.

Motivation Management Service (theMMS.com). *New
York Times* best-selling author Dr. Cherie Carter Scott and
her sister Lynn Stewart are my intuitive coaching mentors.
They have been leaders in the coaching field since 1975
and are experts on how to get past negativity, blocked
feelings, and the barriers to finding your authentic self.

Books by Timothy Gallwey: *The Inner Game of Tennis, The Inner Game of Golf,* and *Inner Skiing.* Sports coach and business consultant with a profound and practical understanding of the power of intuition.

You Can't Afford the Luxury of a Negative Thought—A Book for People with Any Life-Threatening Illness Including Life by Peter McWilliams. A comprehensive encyclopedia on positive thinking endorsed by both Oprah Winfrey and Larry King.

Books by Frederick Dodson: Here is an excerpt from the back of his recent book, *Intuition Training:* "As humans evolve to their next higher version, they will live more from intuition than the old body-mind reactions. Contrary to popular belief, intuition is more accurate than any other source. I owe much of my own success and happiness to it. Many of my decisions are made in contradiction to normal reasoning. The purpose of this book is to look at intuition from many different angles so that you attain a clear sense of this precious gift and take a leap to higher consciousness.

S ID WALKER has been a peak performance sales coach, author, and speaker for more than thirty years. He has coached a wide variety of occupations including Fortune 500 executives with a specialty in intangible sales (financial advisors, consultants, anyone selling a service). A champion of the low-key approach to selling, he believes your objective should be to help your client figure out what he or she wants and then help them get that. Sid has helped created some of the biggest producers in the financial services business with this non-aggressive approach.

In the process of teaching thousands of people the low-key approach to selling, Sid developed a way to help his clients stay "in the Zone." Most people relate to the amazing experience of being in the Zone, when you are totally focused on what you are doing in a relaxed way. The critical voice of the ego disappears and you focus on doing what feels intuitively right moment by moment. In this state, whatever you do seems to work, often in ways you have never experienced before.

What Sid describes as the secret to working in the Zone, and his biggest breakthrough in his coaching practice, is to understand how the ego works to sabotage our progress and maintain the status quo. This is why change is so hard for most people. We are programmed by the ego to resist real change at all costs. You must learn to recognize the logical yet suspect voice of the ego and, most important, you must learn to ignore that voice.

This skill opens the door to being able to hear the quieter voice of your intuition, a required skill for being in the Zone. Furthermore, the only way to conquer all barriers to peak performance is to learn how to stay in the Zone. It is easier than you might think, but it does take guts to go against the ego's conventional wisdom and trust your intuitive instincts. The good news is that being in the Zone is a lot more fun and profitable. Sid has dedicated his coaching to teaching people how to stay in the Zone and create the regular miracles that are the natural result of this approach.

OPT IN TO MAILING LIST

If you would like invitations to *free webinars, periodic articles,* and *new product announcements,* opt in to our mailing list at:

LivingInTheZone.info

Privacy Policy: We will not give out your email or contact information for any reason. You can cancel your subscription at any time.

OTHER BOOKS BY SIDNEY C. WALKER

NONFICTION

HOW I CONQUERED CALL RELUCTANCE, FEAR OF SELF-PROMOTION & INCREASED MY PROSPECTING!

TRUST YOUR GUT—How to Overcome the Obstacles to Greater Success and Self-Fulfillment

HOW TO DOUBLE YOUR SALES BY ASKING A FEW MORE QUESTIONS—Making More Sales by Helping People Get What THEY Really Want

THE PROSPECTING MENTALITY—How to Overcome Call Reluctance, Procrastination, and Sleepless Nights

HOW TO GET MORE COMFORTABLE ASKING FOR REFERRALS

VISIONARY FICTION

THE LIGHTSPACE ULTIMATUM—EVOLVE OR DIE

Hire Sid as Your Coach

Dear Reader,

The reason you hire a skilled coach is to substantially shorten the time required to reach a goal or vision. I can cut years off the learning curve for getting you in the Zone and enjoying this miraculous approach to life.

Learning to get in the Zone is relatively easy. The challenge is staying in the Zone. As soon as the ego perceives you are moving into an unknown area (potential change or risk), it will try to talk you out of whatever you are considering. That's where a coach can come in handy. After a series of conversations and experiences of making the shift back into the Zone, your confidence will grow, and your positive results will keep you going for more.

My coaching practice has been predominantly helping people develop a low-key approach to sales and self-promotion. I have coached financial advisors, consultants, sales reps, entrepreneurs, business owners, executives, professionals, career changers, and retiring professional athletes. The process of learning to live in the Zone is of benefit to anyone regardless of occupation. I expect to have new clients from all walks of life from this book.

The coaching program to teach you to be skilled at living in the Zone does not require a long-term coaching commitment. You can make a lot of progress talking weekly for a couple of months. Then decide how much follow-up coaching you want after that.

If you want to explore the possibility of working together, send me an email with your contact info (Sid@SidWalker.com) so we can set up a time to talk. We can get to know each other a little and see if we might be a good match for a coaching project.

There is no experience in life more empowering than living in the Zone, and you already know that.

Kind regards,

Sid@SidWalker.com

44397071R10076

Made in the USA
Middletown, DE
07 May 2019